UNDERSTANDING ELECTRONICS
3rd Edition

UNDERSTANDING ELECTRONICS
3rd Edition

By R. H. Warring

Edited by G. Randy Slone

TAB Books
Division of McGraw-Hill, Inc.
New York San Francisco Washington, D.C. Auckland Bogotá
Caracas Lisbon London Madrid Mexico City Milan
Montreal New Delhi San Juan Singapore
Sydney Tokyo Toronto

© 1989 by **TAB Books**.
TAB Books is a division of McGraw-Hill, Inc.

pbk   13 14 15 16 17 18 FGR/FGR 9 9 8 7
hc   1 2 3   4   5   6   7   8   9 FGR/FGR 8 7 6 5 4 3 2 1 0 9

Library of Congress Cataloging-in-Publication Data

Warring, R. H. (Ronald Horace), 1920 – 1984
    Understanding electronics / by R.H. Warring. — 3rd ed. / edited
by G. Randy Slone.
      p.   cm.
    Includes index.
    ISBN 0-8306-9044-1   ISBN 0-8306-9344-0 (pbk.)
    1. Electronics—Amateurs' manuals. I. Slone, G. Randy.
II. Title.
TK9965.W39 1989
621.381—dc19   88-32308
                                            CIP

Edited by Alyson Grupp
Cover design: Lori E. Schlosser

Contents

Preface to Third Edition

Understanding Electronics was originally written as a basic guide for home builders of electronic circuits with a particular emphasis on components, how they work, and how they go together to make complete circuits. The aim was to make circuit diagrams more understandable and also set down the "facts and figures" to undertake original circuit design, or to design simple basic circuits from scratch.

Judging by reader response, it has succeeded in this and has also raised many further queries and problems. The third edition has been expanded to cover these and other subjects, to increase both the scope and usefulness of the book. At the same time the opportunity has been taken to revise and update as necessary all the original material retained.

In particular, the not-so-expert electronic hobbyist should find the new Chapter 15, *Transistor Characteristics,* especially helpful and worth studying in some detail. There are also new chapters on amplifiers and oscillators, again expanding the coverage of the original book, and more information on power supplies, particularly those designed for high-voltage applications. A chapter introducing microprocessors has been included together with a considerable number of new illustrations and circuit diagrams.

Finally, an entirely new appendix includes the most frequently used electronic equations. You will find yourself referring to this handy list often.

Introduction

If you find electronics difficult to understand, then you are among the vast majority! One good reason for this difficulty is that you cannot "see" how electronic circuits work; you can only switch them on and hope that they do work. Home construction of electronic circuits might seem something of a gamble, which is not helped by the fact that the "plans" are usually in the form of theoretical circuit diagrams, with components designated by symbols instead of their physical shape and size, and quite probably looking nothing like their arrangement on a practical working circuit.

Take heart! In at least nine cases out of ten, if a circuit built to a published plan does not work, it is for one of two simple reasons: connections are either poorly made or they are made to the wrong components. The only mystery about that is that it happens—even to experts.

The study of electronic circuits is a study of electronic components and the way they behave when connected together in various ways. This book sets out to explain in simple easy-to-understand fashion, without any difficult mathematical calculations or theoretical explanations, what electronic components are, what they look like, what they do, and what sort of circuits they are used in. A basic groundwork in the practical side of simple electronics—and the subject can be quite simple. To make the subject more realistic, there are 51 suggested working circuits to build or experiment with.

There are still the questions of how to read and understand circuit drawings and how to turn them into practical working circuits, so separate chapters are devoted to these two particular subjects. There is also a chapter on printed-circuit construction.

Because most simple electronic circuits are battery powered, the subject of different battery types and their performances is also covered in some detail. Also included are circuits for building a battery charger, either to operate off the mains or from a car battery.

Understanding Electronics 3rd Edition should be an excellent starter for anyone wanting to take up practical electronics as a hobby interest — and an ideal reference to make the types and construction of more elaborate circuits described in more advanced books and monthly journals more understandable. It should prove invaluable as a source of information that has been left out of other electronic books on an author's assumption that "everyone should know that." In fact, such books are often described as "too technical" or "too advanced." This present book should fill that particular gap.

List of Working Circuits

1
Units,
Abbreviations, and Symbols

In electronics there are six basic *units* to measure quantities which define what is going on in a circuit. Here are the first three, with the letter symbols used as abbreviations:

Volts (V)—A measure of the potential, *emf* (electromotive force), or *voltage* in a circuit. For practical purposes, potential difference, *emf*, and voltage all really mean the same thing.
Amps (A)—A measure of the *current* flowing in a circuit.
Watts (W)—A measure of the *power* developed by the flow of current through a circuit.

The other three refer to the effect of components in the circuit:

Ohms (Ω)—A measure of the *resistance* or individual resistances in a circuit when the current flow is direct (*dc*).
Farads (F)—A measure of the *capacitance* present in a circuit or produced by individual components; i.e., capacitors.
Henrys (H)—A measure of the *inductance* present in a circuit or produced by individual components such as coils.

Two other important quantities, both of which are measured in ohms, are:

Impedance (Z)—A measure of the effective resistance or individual resistances in a circuit when the current flow is alternating (*ac*).
Reactance (X)—The combined effect of inductance and capacitance in an *ac* circuit.

Capital letters are also used as abbreviations for voltage and current. Strictly speaking E (for *emf*) is the correct symbol for a voltage source, with V (for volts) in other parts of the circuit. V_s can be used instead of E for a source voltage. The capital letter I is used for current. In some circuits lowercase letters are used to indicate voltages and currents flowing in different parts of a circuit; e.g., v and i, respectively. These may have a reference annotation attached, particularly in the case of transistor circuits; e.g., v_e, describing emitter voltage.

The relationship between units is explained in Chapter 3. There are also various other units employed in electronics, the use and meaning of which will be made clear in appropriate chapters.

In practical circuits, numerical values of these units may be very large, or very small. Resistance values, for example, may run to millions of ohms. Capacitor values may be in millionths or even million-millionths of a farad. To avoid writing out such values in full, prefixes are used to designate the number associated with the particular value involved. Normally, the symbol rather than the full prefix is used,

mega (M) — ×1,000,000
kilo (k) — ×1,000
milli (m) — divided by 1,000 (or 1/1,000th)
micro (μ) — divided by 1,000,000 (or 1/1,000,000th)
nano (n) — divided by 1,000,000,000 (or 1/1,000,000,000th)
pico (p) — divided by 1,000,000,000,000 (or 1/1,000,000,000,000)

For example, instead of writing out 22,000,000 ohms, it is shown as 22 Mohms, or 22 MΩ, using symbols both for the prefix and basic unit. Similarly a capacitor value of 0.000,000,000,220 farads is shown as 220 picoF, or, more usually 220 pF.

The *multipliers* (M and k) are most commonly associated with values of *resistors,* and also for specifying radio frequencies. The lowest *divisor* (m) is most usually associated with the values of *current* typical of transistor circuits, etc. It is also used to specify most practical values of inductances. The larger *divisors* (μ, n, and p) are most commonly associated with capacitor values.

Single capital letter abbreviations are also used for components. The main ones are:

C — capacitors
D — diodes
L — coils
R — resistors

These are all standard and universally accepted abbreviations. With other components this is not always the case. Thus transistors may be designed T, TR, Tr, VT or even Q on circuits originating from different sources. The use of TR, Tr, or Q is preferred, leaving the letter T as the abbreviation for transformers. Note the abbreviation FET (or fet) is used for a *field-effect transistor* in text, although it may be "Q" in diagrams.

In practical circuits, more than one of the same type of components are

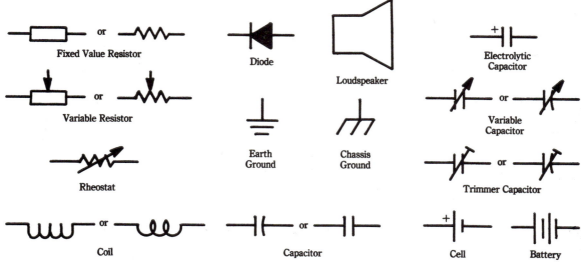

Fig. 1-1. Symbols for basic circuit components. Other symbols are given in later chapters.

normally used. Individual components of the same type are then designated by numbers (usually reading from left to right across the circuit) associated with the component *symbol* (Fig. 1-1). See also Chapter 3. Thus resistors are designated R1, R2, R3; capacitors C1, C2, C3; and so on. There is no correct or specific sequence in which such numbers are allocated. They are there only to identify a particular component.

Here are some other general abbreviations that are widely used, although again they may be shown in various different ways: capital letters, or lowercase letters in upright or italic, with or without periods. Thus the abbreviation of alternating current may appear in five different ways:

AC   a.c.   *a.c.*   ac   *ac*

The general preference is that all such abbreviations should be in lowercase without periods, and so the following abbreviations are shown that way:

ac — alternating current
af — audio frequency
agc — automatic gain control
am* — amplitude modulated (or amplitude modulation)
dc — direct current
eht — extra high tension
fm* — frequency modulated (or frequency modulation)
hf — high frequency
ht — high tension

---

* There is a good reason for retaining capital letters for these abbreviations, since AM and FM radios use them this way.

ic — integrated circuits
if — intermediate frequency (also i-f)
if — low frequency
rf — radio frequency
uhf — ultra high frequency
vhf — very high frequency

2
DC and AC

A basic direct current (dc) circuit is simple enough to understand. A source of electrical force (such as a battery) is connected via wires to various components with a return path to the source. Current then flows through the circuit in a particular direction. Figure 2-1 shows a very elementary circuit of this type where a battery is connected to a dc electric motor and is compared with a similar closed loop hydraulic motor in a simple recirculating system.

It is obvious what happens in the hydraulic circuit. The pump is a source of pressurized water which impinges on the vanes of the hydraulic motor to drive it. There is a flow of water around the system. At the same time, there is some loss of pressure energy due to the friction of the water flowing through the pipes and the motor. This is the resistance in the circuit. But most of the pressure energy delivered by the pump is converted into power by the hydraulic motor.

In the electrical circuit counterpart, the battery is a source of *electrical* pressure (which in simple terms we designate *voltage*). This forces an electrical *current* to flow through the circuit, opposed by the *resistance* offered by the wiring and the electric motor coils. Again, most of the original electrical energy in the battery is converted into power by the electric motor. Provided the battery voltage does not change, a constant value of current will flow through the circuit always in the same direction, and the electric motor will continue to run at a constant speed.

Conventionally, dc current flow is regarded as being from the positive to the negative terminals of a battery or any other dc source (such as a dynamo). It is a

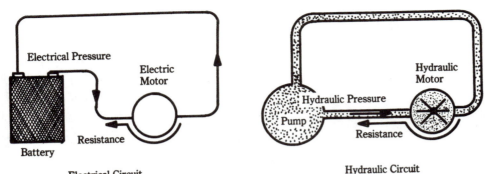

Electrical Pressure

Electric Motor

Resistance

Battery

Electrical Circuit

Hydraulic Motor

Hydraulic Pressure

Pump

Resistance

Hydraulic Circuit

Fig. 2-1. An electrical circuit is similar to a hydraulic circuit.

stream flow, just like the water flow in the hydraulic circuit, but the stream is actually composed of sub-atomic particles or *electrons.* Unfortunately, after convention had established the positive to negative flow definition, it was found that this electron stream flow was actually from *negative to positive.* This does not matter for most practical purposes, but for an understanding of how transistors and other solid-state devices work it is necessary to appreciate this "reverse" working.

Positive always seems stronger than negative, so it is difficult to think of current as flowing other than from positive to negative. We can relate this to electrons flowing from negative to positive by thinking of electrons as particles of negative electricity. Being "weaker" (negative), they represent a reverse flow, setting up conditions for a *positive* flow of current—from *positive to negative.* Otherwise, simply forget the difference and work on the practical fact that + and — are only terms of convenience used to ensure that components in a circuit which have positive and negative sides are connected up correctly. This applies mainly to batteries, transistors, diodes, and electrolytic capacitors.

All materials are composed of atoms in which there is a stable balance of positive and negative charges (except in the atoms of radioactive elements). The application of an electrical pressure causes electrons to be displaced from the atom, leaving it with an effective positive charge. It is then in a state to attract any stray electrons. Since there is electrical pressure present, this means that there is a movement of electrons along the chain of atoms comprising the wiring and component(s) in the complete return circuit. It is this movement that constitutes the electric current flowing through the circuit, the strength of the current being dependent on the number of electrons passing any particular point in the circuit in a given time. Break the circuit and the pressure is broken, so current flow ceases. So, in fact, the analogy with a hydraulic circuit is not really valid in this instance (the hydraulic pump still delivers water under pressure if its circuit is broken until it has emptied the fluid in the circuit between the break and the pump).

Atoms of materials like metals will give up electrons readily when subject to electrical pressure, and so make good *conductors* of electricity. Atoms of most non-metals, including plastics, are reluctant to give up electrons even under high

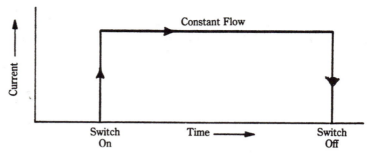

Fig. 2-2. Direct current flow with constant circuit resistance.

electrical pressure, and so are essentially nonconductors. If materials are extremely resistant to giving up atoms, they are classified as *insulators*.

Summarizing, then, a dc circuit when connected or switched on provides a constant flow of current in one direction through the circuit as in Fig. 2-2, unless something changes in the circuit (e.g., source voltage changes, or a circuit resistance value alters). The value of this current is determined by the source voltage and the total resistance in the circuit (see Chapter 3). Current flow is also regarded as positive (or positive current).

In the case of an ac circuit, the source of electrical pressure continually reverses in a periodic manner. This means that current flows through the circuit first in one direction (positive) and then the other (negative). In other words, a simple graph of current flow with time will look like Fig. 2-3. The swing from maximum positive to maximum negative is known as the *amplitude* of an ac current. Also one complete period from zero to maximum positive, back to zero, down to maximum negative and back to zero again is known as a *cycle*. These cycles may occur at varying rates from a few times a second to millions of times a second and define the *frequency* of the ac current, frequency being equal to the number of cycles per second. In the case of the domestic mains supply (in Britain), for example, the frequency is 50 cycles-per-second, or 60 cycles-per-second in the U.S. But "cycles-per-second" is an obsolete term. It is now called hertz (abbreviated Hz). Thus standard mains frequency is 50 or 60 Hz.

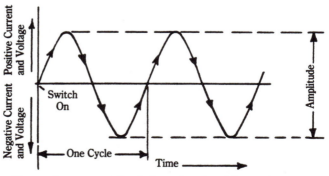

Fig. 2-3. Alternating current flow is in cycles of positive and negative current.

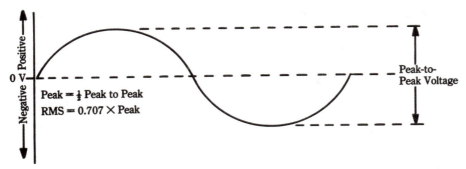

Peak = ½ Peak to Peak
RMS = 0.707 × Peak

Peak-to-Peak Voltage

Fig. 2-4. Peak-to-peak, peak, and root mean square voltages defined and compared.

Apart from the fact that ac is continually swinging from positive to negative current flow, the other difference is that the actual current value present is also changing all the time. It does, however, have an "average" value which can be defined in various ways. The usual one is the Root Mean Square (or *rms*), which is equal to 0.7071 times the maximum cycle values for sine wave ac such as normally generated by an alternator, Fig. 2-4. Alternating current may, however, be generated with other types of waveform.

Another characteristic of ac is that both the voltage *and* current are continually changing in similar cycles. Only rarely, however, do the voltage and current both attain maximum and zero values at exactly the same time. In other words the current (waveform) curve is displaced relative to the voltage (waveform) curve, Fig. 2-5. This displacement is known as a *phase difference.* It is normally expressed in terms of the ratio of the actual displacement to a full cycle length on the zero line, multiplied by 360 (since a full cycle represents 360 degrees of ac working). This is called the *phase angle.* Usually the current will "peak" after the voltage (i.e., be displaced to the right of the diagram), whereupon the current is said to be lagging and the phase angle is referred to as *angle of lag.*

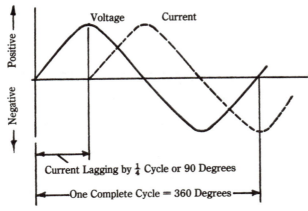

Current Lagging by ¼ Cycle or 90 Degrees

One Complete Cycle = 360 Degrees

Fig. 2-5. Current usually lags behind voltage in an alternating current circuit.

8

The use of the term "angle" can be a bit confusing at first. It is really a matter of mathematical convenience, useful in more complicated calculations involving vector diagrams. For a general understanding of ac it is better to think of angle as meaning a particular "number point" on a line length representing one full cycle divided into 360 divisions. Thus a phase angle of 30 degrees can be understood as a point 30/360ths along that line.

Phase difference (phase angle) can be an important factor in the design and working of many alternating current circuits because when a current lags (or leads) the voltage, the timing aspects of a circuit are affected.

3
Basic Circuits and Circuit Laws

As noted in Chapter 2, the current which flows in a simple dc circuit is dependent on the applied voltage and the resistance in the circuit. Voltage can be measured directly by a *voltmeter* placed across the battery (or dc source) terminals; and *current* by an *ammeter* connected in *series* in the circuit, as in Fig. 3-1. This diagram also shows the circuit components in symbolic form.

OHM'S LAW

The relationship between voltage (E), current (I), and resistance (R) is given by Ohm's law:

$$I = \frac{E}{R}$$

In plain language:

$$amps = \frac{volts}{resistance\ in\ ohms}$$

or the formula can be rewritten:

$$volts = amps \times ohms$$

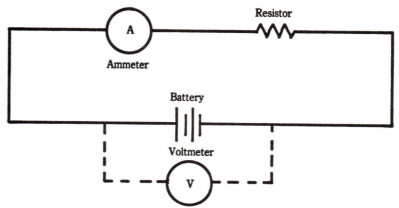

Fig. 3-1. Basic dc circuit shown in two ways, with meters for measuring current and voltage indicated.

$$\text{ohms} = \frac{\text{volts}}{\text{amps}}$$

This is one of the most basic and most useful laws of electronics and is equally applicable to ac circuits which are purely resistive (i.e., do not have additional resistance effects produced by the current being alternating rather than steady).

Ohm's law makes it possible to calculate (and thus design) the performance of a simple dc circuit. For example, suppose you need a current of 200 milliamps (mA) to flow in a particular circuit to be powered by a 6-volt battery. Using Ohm's law, the corresponding circuit resistance required to give this current can easily be worked out:

$$\text{ohms} = \frac{\text{volts}}{\text{amps}} = \frac{6}{0.200}$$
$$= 30 \text{ ohms}$$

Components are connected by wires, but the resistance of wiring is small enough to be negligible. Thus in a simple dc circuit it is the effective total of all the resistor values and other components which offer resistance. Just what this total value is depends on how the various resistors which may be present are connected (see Chapter 4).

In some cases it is easy to calculate the resistance of a typical load. For example, a flashlight bulb is usually rated by volts and the current it draws. Ohm's law can then be used to find its nominal resistance. For example, if a bulb is rated at 6 volts and 50 mA, from Ohm's law:

$$\text{Resistance} = \frac{6}{0.05} = 120 \text{ ohms.}$$

There is just one snag to this method of estimating load resistance. With filament bulbs, for example, the specified current drawn refers to the bulb in working conditions with the filament heated up. Its actual resistance initially when the filament is cold can be considerably lower, drawing more current through the bulb. This may, or may not, be a disadvantage in a particular circuit. Also, there are other types of loads, like dc electric motors, where the effective resistance varies condiserably with the speed at which the motor is running. Initially, such a motor will have a very low resistance; its effective resistance then increases with speed.

Two other basic relationships also apply in a simple dc circuit:

1. The *current* value is the same through every part of the circuit, unless a part of the circuit involves parallel-connected paths.

Thus, in a circuit (A) of Fig. 3-2, all the resistors in the circuit are connected in series so that the same current will flow through each resistor.

In circuit (B) of Fig. 3-2, the resistors are connected in parallel. In this case each resistor represents a separate path for the current and the value of current flowing through each leg depends on the value of that resistor. These current values can be calculated from Ohm's law:

$$\text{through resistor 1, current} = \frac{E}{R1}$$

$$\text{through resistor 2, current} = \frac{E}{R2}$$

$$\text{through resistor 3, current} = \frac{E}{R3}$$

The current flowing through the wiring part of the circuit is the sum of these three currents; i.e.,

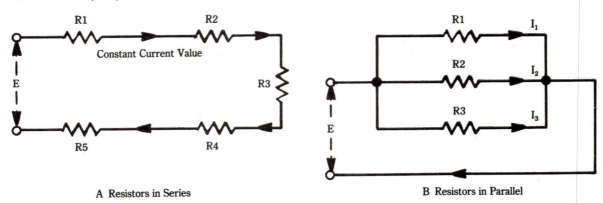

A Resistors in Series

B Resistors in Parallel

Fig. 3-2. Current has the same value through all resistors connected in series, but is different through each resistor connected in parallel.

$$\frac{E}{R1} + \frac{E}{R2} + \frac{E}{R3} \quad \text{or E} \quad \frac{1}{R1} + \frac{1}{R2} + \frac{1}{R3}$$

2. The voltage throughout a simple dc circuit is not constant but suffers a drop across each resistor.

This can be illustrated by the circuit shown in Fig. 3-3, where the voltages across the individual resistors are calculated (or measured with a voltmeter) as V1, V2 and V3. The total resistance in the circuit is R1 + R2 + R3.

The current (which is the same throughout the circuit) is given by:

$$I = \frac{E}{R1 + R2 + R3}$$

We then have the conditions:

V1, measured across R1 = current × resistance
= I × R1

V2, measured across R2 = I × R2

V3, measured across R3 = I × R3

Each of these voltages is less than E.

Comparison with a hydraulic circuit again (see Chapter 2) can help understand how a resistor works as a voltage dropper. In a hydraulic circuit, pressure is analogous to voltage in an electronic circuit. The equivalent to a resistor is some device restricting fluid flow—say a partially closed valve. Flow through this resistor produces a pressure drop. Similarly, the flow of electricity through a resistor produces a voltage drop.

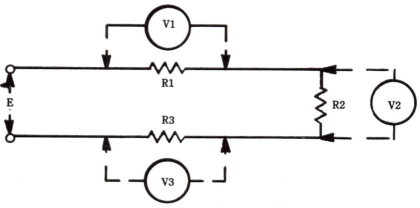

Fig. 3-3. Resistors drop voltage in a dc circuit.

VOLTAGE-DROPPER CIRCUIT

The above is now reworked as a practical example. To power a 6-volt electrical appliance (say a 6-volt transistor radio) from a 12-volt battery. In this case, the appliance is considered as a resistance *load*. To drop the voltage from 12 to 6 across this load, a dropper resistor, R, is required in the circuit shown in Fig. 3-4. It remains to calculate a suitable value for this dropping resistor, but to do this it is necessary to know the effective resistance of the load. (If this is not known it can be measured with an ohmmeter.) Suppose it is 100 ohms.

Using Ohm's law again, if this load is to have 6 volts applied across it, and its resistance is 100 ohms, the current required to flow through the circuit is:

$$1 = \frac{6}{100}$$
$$= 0.06 \text{ amps (60 milliamps)}$$

This same current flows through the rest of the circuit. This, considering the circuit from the 12-volt end:

$$\text{total resistance required} = \frac{12}{0.06}$$
$$= 200 \text{ ohms}$$

The load already contributed 100 ohms, so the value of dropping resistor required must be $200 - 100 = 100$ ohms. A further calculation shows the voltage drop across this resistor:

$$V = 0.06 \times 100$$
$$= 6 \text{ volts}$$

This particular example also demonstrates another simple rule concerning dropping resistors. If the voltage is to be halved, then the value of the dropping resistor required is the same as that of the load.

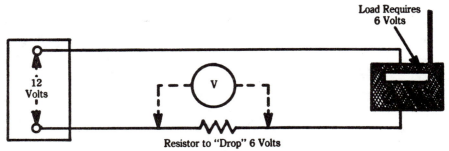

Fig. 3-4. *Practical application of a dropping resistor.*

POWER IN THE CIRCUIT

The power developed in a circuit by virtue of the electrical pressure (volts) and resulting current flow (amps) is given by the product of these two values, and measured in *watts*. Thus:

$$power = watts = volts \times amps$$

This same definition applies both to dc and ac circuits.

Power is used up in producing a useful result in making the circuit work (whether this be operating a radio, driving an electric motor, heating an electric element, etc.). But all components which have resistance absorb a certain amount of power which is waste power normally dissipated in the form of heat. No practical device can work without some resistance in the circuit, and thus some power loss is inevitable. More important, the heating effect must not be so great that the component is damaged. Thus components normally have a *power rating* which should not be exceeded. In specific cases, even when operating within their power rating, provision may have to be made to conduct heat away from the component — as in the case of heatsinks used with power transistors.

Referring to the example of the dropping resistor, this definitely wastes power to the tune of 6 (volts) $\times$ 0.06 (amps) = 0.36 watts. To be on the safe side, therefore, the resistor chosen would need to have a power rating of at least ½ watt, and would also have to be placed in a position where it receives adequate ventilation to prevent heat build-up in the surrounding air.

The majority of transistor circuits work on low voltages, with low current values, and so components with quite moderate power ratings are usually adequate. Circuits carrying higher voltages and currents demand the use of components with correspondingly higher power ratings, and often need even more attention to ventilation. Thus, the actual value of a component is only part of its specification. Its power rating can be equally important.

Note that since $V = IR$, power can also be calculated as:

$$watts = (current)^2 \times resistance$$

$$P = I^2R$$

This is often a more convenient formula for calculating power in a particular part of a circuit.

SHUNT CIRCUITS

A shunt circuit is used to drop a current flowing through a particular component. It normally comprises two resistances in parallel, one resistance being the component resistance and the other the shunt resistance. The appropriate value of the shunt resistance is again calculated directly from Ohm's law.

A typical example of the use of a shunt resistance is to adapt an ammeter movement to measure different current ranges (as in a multimeter). In this case the load resistance is that of the coil of the ammeter, which is initially designed to give a full-scale deflection with a particular current flowing through it (call this I_1). The instrument cannot measure any higher current than I_1 since this would simply tend to carry the pointer past its full deflection, and very likely cause damage. Thus, the meter is designed to handle the lowest current range required, and a shunt resistor (or a series of shunt resistors) added which can be switched into the meter circuit to extend the range. Figure 3-5 shows this arrangement with just one shunt resistor connected for switching into the circuit.

If the shunt resistor is to extend the ammeter range to a higher current, I_2, giving full-scale deflection, then the required value of the shunt resistor follows from:

1. Current which has to flow through the shunt is $I_2 - I_1$. This means that a current greater than I_1 will never flow through the meter movement (unless the actual current applied to the meter exceeds I_2).
2. Voltage drops across the meter $= I_1 \times R_m$ (where R_m is the resistance of the meter).
3. Shunt resistance required is therefore:

$$\frac{\text{voltage drop across instrument}}{\text{current flow through shunt}} = \frac{I_1 \times R_m}{I_2 - I_1}$$

Again, there is a simple rule to follow if the current range of the meter is to be doubled. In this case the shunt resistance required is the same as that of the meter.

AMMETER INTO VOLTMETER

An ammeter, which is an instrument used for measuring current, can also be made to measure volts by connecting a resistor in *series* with the meter — Fig. 3-6. This, in fact, is another example of a voltage dropper. Again, if the maximum meter current for full-scale deflection is I_1, the *total* resistance which must be in circuit is:

$$\text{total } R = \frac{V}{I_1}$$

where V is the voltage range it is desired to measure.

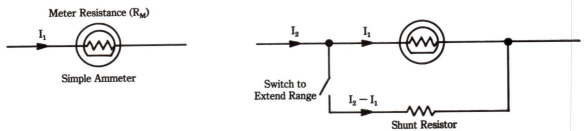

Fig. 3-5. *Extending the range of a milliammeter.*

The value of the series resistor required is this total resistance *less* the resistance of the meter (the latter may be negligible in comparison with the value of series resistor required and its likely tolerance—see Chapter 4).

Again, several series resistors may be used, switched into the circuit individually to provide different voltage-measuring ranges on the meter movement, as shown in the right hand diagram of Fig. 3-6.

DIVIDERS

A voltage divider is yet another example of the practical application of a voltage dropper. The basic circuit is shown in Fig. 3-7, and since the current flow through R1 and R2 is the same, the following voltage values apply:

$$V1 = \text{source voltage (e.g., battery voltage)}$$

$$V2 = V1 \times R1$$

$$V3 = \frac{V1}{R1 + R2} \times R2$$

$$\left(\text{Note: } \frac{V1}{R1 + R2} \text{ is the current flowing through R1 and R2} \right).$$

It follows that by suitable selection of values for R1 and R2, virtually any lower voltage than V1 can be tapped from points A and B, or B and C (or both). It also has the advantage that it is not necessary to know the load resistance before suitable dropper resistances can be calculated. It could thus be a more practical alternative for the example described in Fig. 3-4, but connection to a load does, of course, result in a further drop in voltage.

If the resistance of the load is known, then there is no particular problem with a fixed resistor voltage divider. Calculate the value of R2 (Fig. 3-7) on the basis of no load resistance, then subtract the actual value of the load resistance from this to arrive at the required value for R2. (In the complete tapped circuit, R2 and the load resistance is effectively in series.)

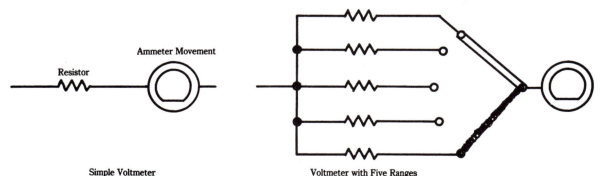

Fig. 3-6. Converting an ammeter into a voltmeter.

Simple Voltmeter   Voltmeter with Five Ranges

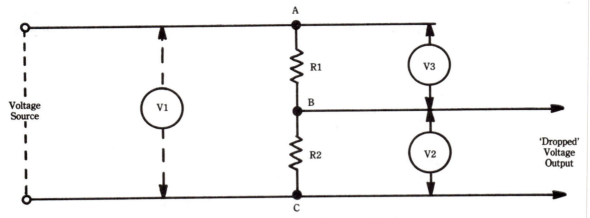

Fig. 3-7. Basic potential divider circuit.

BASIC AC CIRCUITS

As explained in Chapter 2, the voltage and current flow both alternate in ac circuits, with the possibility of one leading or lagging the other. Also, it was intimated that the effective resistance offered by resistance components may be modified (usually increased) by reactive effects. These effects become increasingly marked as the *frequency* of the ac increases, and at radio frequencies are more pronounced than pure resistance.

It is possible to obtain an ac circuit which is purely resistive, particularly at lower frequencies, in which case Ohm's law is equally valid for such circuits as it is for dc circuits. Ohm's law can also be applied to ac circuits in which reactive effects are present, but in slightly modified form. These reactive effects are described specifically as *reactance* and *impedance*.

Reactance is the circuit loading effect produced by *capacitors* and *inductances* (coils). It is measured in ohms and designated by the symbol X. Its actual value is dependent both on the component value and the frequency of the ac.

In the case of capacitors, capacitive reactance (usually designated X_c) is given by:

$$X_c = \frac{1}{2\pi f C}$$

where f is the ac frequency in Hz, C is the capacitance in farads, and $\pi = 3.1412$.

In the case of inductances, *inductive reactance* (usually designated X_L) is given by:

$$X_L = 2\pi f L$$

where L is the inductance in henrys

If the ac circuit contains only reactance (i.e., does not have any separate resistance), then X takes the place of resistance (R) in the Ohm's law formula:

$$I = \frac{E}{X}$$

In practice, reactance present is also usually associated with resistance, the resulting combination representing the *impedance* (Z) of the circuit.

If reactance and resistance are in series:

$$Z = \sqrt{R^2 + X^2}$$

If reactance and resistance are in parallel:

$$Z = \sqrt{\frac{RX}{R^2 + X^2}}$$

Again, impedance (Z) takes the place of resistance in the Ohm's law formula:

$$I = \frac{E}{Z}$$

These are the basic formulas for ac circuit calculations.

POWER FACTOR

Power factor is something specific to ac circuits, although it is only the resistance in such circuits that actually consume power. This power consumed can be calculated as the product of the square of the current flowing through the resistance and the value of the resistance; i.e., I^2R watts. The apparent power in the circuit is the product of ac voltage and current, correctly specified as volt-amps.

The ratio of the power consumed to the apparent power is called the *power factor,* usually expressed as a percentage. If the circuit is purely resistive, then the power factor is 100 percent (since all the apparent power is consumed in the resistance). Reactance does not consume power, so in a purely reactive circuit the power factor is zero. When a circuit contains both resistance and impedance (i.e., reactance), then the power factor is always less than 100 percent, its value depending on the resistance present.

DC and AC in the Same Circuit

It is quite possible to have both dc and ac flowing in the same circuit. In fact, this is the principle on which most radio and similar circuits work. The dc is the basic source of electrical supply, on which various ac currents are superimposed. The one essential difference is that dc can only flow through a continuous circuit,

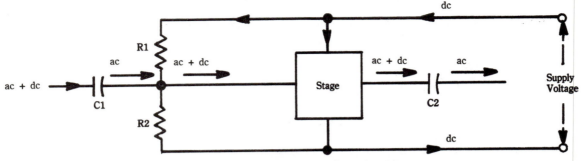

Fig. 3-8. Flow of ac and dc in a circuit.

whereas ac can pass through components such as capacitors which present a break in the circuit to dc. These effects can be used to advantage to isolate stages in a circuit.

In the type of circuit shown in Fig. 3-8, for example, an input comprising a mixture of dc and ac is applied to the left-hand side of the circuit. If only the ac component of the signal is required, the dc content can be blocked by a capacitor (C1). Meantime, the next part of the circuit which has to deal with that signal is powered by dc from the source supply (say a battery), probably via resistors R1 and R2 acting as dividers to get the voltages correct for that stage (other stages may need different working dc voltages, all coming from the same source). The output signal from this stage then consists of a mixture of dc and ac. If only the ac content is wanted for passing to the next stage, a capacitor (C2) is again used as a block for dc.

4
Resistors

Resistors, as the name implies, are designed to provide some desirable, or necessary, amount of *resistance* to current flow in a circuit. They can also be used to drop voltages, as explained in chapter 3. As such, they are the main elements used in circuit design to arrive at the desired current flows and voltages that work the circuit. Resistors do not generate electrical energy, but merely absorb it. This energy is dissipated in the form of heat. The performance of a resistor is not affected by frequency, so it behaves in the same way in both dc and ac circuits. (There are exceptions, as noted later.)

Resistors are specified by (a) resistance value in ohms; (b) tolerance as a percentage of the nominal value; and (c) power rating in watts. They are also categorized by the type of construction.

COLOR CODE

Resistance value and tolerance are normally indicated by a color code consisting of four colored rings, starting at, or close to, one end (Fig. 4-1). These are read as follows:

    1st ring gives first digit
    2nd ring gives second digit
    3rd ring gives number of zeros to put after first two digits

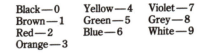

Black — 0	Yellow — 4	Violet — 7
Brown — 1	Green — 5	Grey — 8
Red — 2	Blue — 6	White — 9
Orange — 3		

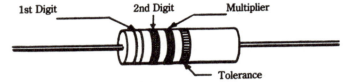

Fig. 4-1. Standard resistor color code marking.

The fourth colored ring gives the tolerance:

silver — 10% tolerance either side of the nominal value
gold — 5% tolerance either side of the nominal value
red — 2% tolerance either side of the nominal value
brown — 1% tolerance either side of the nominal value

Example: Resistor color code read as brown, blue, orange.

	Brown	Blue	Orange
Value read as	1	6	000

i.e., 16,000 Ω or 16 kΩ (kilohms).

Absence of a fourth ring implies a tolerance of 20 percent.

Certain types of modern resistors of larger physical size may have letters and numbers marked on the body instead of colored rings. With this coding, the numbers indicate the numerical value and the following letter the multiplier, where:

E = × 1
K = × 1,000 (or kilohms)
M = × 1,000,000 (or megohms)

A second letter then gives the tolerance:

M = 20% tolerance either side of the nominal value
K = 10% tolerance either side of the nominal value
J = 5% tolerance either side of the nominal value
H = 2.5% tolerance either side of the nominal value
G = 2% tolerance either side of the nominal value
F = 1% tolerance either side of the nominal value

The actual range of (nominal) resistance values to which resistors are made is based on steps that give an approximately constant *percentage* change in resistance from one value to the next — not simple arithmetical steps like 1, 2, 3, etc. These are based on the preferred numbers:

1, 1.2, 1.5, 1.8, 2.2, 2.7, 3.3, 3.9, 4.7, 5.6, 6.8, 8.2, 10, 12, 15, 18, etc.

Thus, for example, a typical range of resistor values would be:

10, 12, 15, 18, 22, 27, 33, 39, 47, 56, 68, 82, and 100 ohms
120, 150, 180, 220, 270, 330, 390, 470, 560, 680 and 820 ohms
1, 1.2, 1.5, 1.8, 2.2, 2.7, 3.3, 4.7, 5.6, 6.8, and 8.2 kilohms).
10, 12, etc. kilohms
1, 12, etc. megohms

As a general rule, resistors with a 10 percent tolerance are suitable for average circuit use. The actual resistance value of, say, a 1 kilohm resistor would then be anything between 900 and 1,100 ohms. For more critical work, such as radio circuits, resistors with a 5 percent tolerance are preferred. Closer tolerances are not normally required, except for very critical circuits.

POWER RATING

The physical size (or shape) of a resistor provides no clue to its resistance value, but can be a rough guide to its *power rating.* Physical sizes (Fig. 4-2) range from about 4 mm long by 1 mm diameter up to about 50 mm long and 6 mm or more diameter. The former would probably have a power rating of 1/20 watt and the latter possibly 10 watts. More specifically, however, the power rating is related to type as well as size. A general rule that does apply to power rating, however, is that while this figure nominally represents a safe maximum the resistor can tolerate without damage, it is usually best to operate a resistor well below its power rating—say at 50 percent—particularly if components are crowded on a circuit or the circuit is enclosed in a case with little or no ventilation.

VOLTAGE RATING

Maximum operating voltage also can be specified for resistors, but since this is usually of the order of 250 volts or more, this parameter is not important when choosing resistors for battery circuits. Resistors used on mains circuits must, however, have a suitable voltage rating.

Types of Construction

Resistor *types* classified by construction follow.

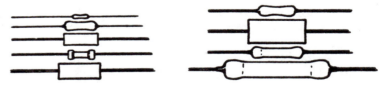

Fig. 4-2. Examples of modern resistor outlines (actual size).

Carbon Resistors (also called carbon-composition, molded-carbon, and carbon rod). Carbon resistors are in the form of a small rod molded from carbon and a binder, with wire connections at each end. The rod is usually protected with a paper or ceramic sleeve, or a lacquer coating. Carbon resistors are the most common (and cheapest) type of resistor, and are available in values from 10 ohms to 22 megohms. Standard types are usually available in ⅛, ¼, ½, 1, and 2 watt ratings.

It is a general characteristic of carbon resistors that their value remains stable at normal temperatures, but above 60°C their resistance increases rapidly with increasing temperature.

Carbon-film Resistors (also known as high-stability carbon resistors). To make a carbon-film resistor, a thin film of carbon is deposited on a small ceramic rod. The rod is fitted with metal end caps, to which wire leads are attached. The body of the resistor is usually protected by a varnish, paint, or silicone resin coating, but some types may be encased in a ceramic, plastic, or glass outer coating.

Carbon-film resistors are little affected by temperature changes (their stability is usually better than 1 percent) and are also characterized by low noise. They are available in sub-miniature sizes (1/20 and 1/10 watt power rating, and in larger sizes up to 1 watt power rating. They are a preferred type for radio circuits, particularly as they have excellent high-frequency characteristics.

Metal-film Resistors. To make a metal-film resistor, a metallic film (usually nickel-chromium) is deposited on a glass or ceramic rod. A helical track is then cut in the film to produce the required resistance value. Metallic end cats are then fitted, carrying the wire leads, and the body is protected by a lacquer, paint, or plastic coating. Stability characteristics are similar to those of carbon-film resistors, but they are more expensive. They are generally produced in miniature sizes with power ratings from 1/10 watt upwards.

Metal-oxide Film Resistors. Construction is similar to that of a metal-film resistor except that the coating used is a metallic oxide (usually tin oxide), subsequently covered with a heat-resistant coating. This type of resistor is virtually impervious to accidental overheating (e.g., when making soldered connections) and is also not affected by dampness. Stability is very high (better than 1 percent), and the power ratings are high for their physical size.

Metal-glaze Resistors. In this type, the resistive film deposited on the rod is a cermet (metal-ceramic); otherwise, construction is similar to metal-film resistors.

Film-resistors also can be classified as *thick-film* or *thin-film*. As a general rule, individual resistors of this type are thick-film. Thick-film resistors are also made in groups on a small substrate and encapsulated in integraded circuit chips. Thin-film resistors are made in a similar way, but on a considerably smaller scale for use in the manufacture of integrated circuits.

Effect of Age

All resistors can be expected to undergo a change in resistance with age. This is most marked in the case of carbon-composition resistors, where the change might be as much as 20 percent in a year or so. In the case of carbon-film and metallic-film resistors, the change seldom will be more than a few percent.

Effect of High Frequencies

The general effect of increasing frequency in ac circuits is to decrease the apparent value of the resistor, and the higher the resistor value the greater this change is likely to be. This effect is most marked with carbon-composition and wire-round resistors. Carbon-film and metal-film resistors all have stable high-frequency characteristics.

WIRE-WOUND RESISTORS

A wire-round resistor is made by wrapping a length of resistance wire around a ceramic coil. The whole is then covered with a protective coating or film. The specific advantages offered by wire resistors are that a wide range of values can be produced (typically from 1 ohm to 300 kilohms) with power ratings from 1 to 50 watts (or up to 225 watts in "power" types) and tolerances as close as 1 percent. They also have excellent stability and low noise. Their disadvantages are that they are most costly and also unsuitable for use in ac circuits carrying high frequencies because their effective value changes. Physically, they need be no bigger than film-type resistors for the same power rating.

VARIABLE RESISTIVE DEVICES

The most common type of variable resistive device used in modern electronics is called a *potentiometer*. A potentiometer is a three-lead resistive device consisting of a fixed resistive element that can be swept by a wiper arm. The fixed resistive element, or *track*, may be circular (usually a 270-degree arc) or a straight line, circular types being the more common.

The resistive element may be wire-wound, carbon-composition, carbon-film, or metallic-film. The former type is known as a wire-wound potentiometer. Carbon-track potentiometers are the cheapest (with the same limitations as carbon-composition resistors), but are available only with moderate power ratings — e.g., ¼ watt for low resistance values — reducing with higher resistance values. Wire-wound potentiometers usually have higher power ratings and are also available in lower resistance values than carbon-track potentiometers. Tolerances are usually on the order of 10 percent of 20 percent, but may be much closer with precision potentiometers.

Connections should be obvious from Fig. 4-3. Thus, with connections to end 1 of the track and the wiper, length 1 to C of the resistive track is in the circuit. Actual circuit resistance thus can be varied by moving the wiper towards 3 (increasing resistance), or toward 1 (decreasing resistance).

The change in resistance can occur *proportionally* to the actual length of track involved, or *logarithmetically*, where there is a logarithmic increase in

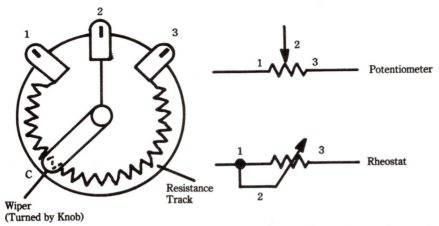

Fig. 4-3. *Potentiometer shown in schematic form (left). Corresponding terminal positions are shown on the symbols (right).*

resistance with wiper movement uncovering more track (similar to the "steps" adopted for standard resistor values). The former is known as a *linear* potentiometer and the latter a *log* potentiometer. Potentiometers can also have characteristics between the two. Note that *linear* in this description has quite a different meaning to a linear physical shape of potentiometer. To avoid confusion, it is best to refer to the latter as a slide-type potentiometer.

There is also a class of variable resistors intended to be adjusted to a particular resistance setting and then left undisturbed. These are known as *trim potentiometers,* or just trim pots. They are small in size and more limited in maximum resistance value—typically from 100 ohms to 1 megohm. They are usually designed for adjustment by a screwdriver applied to the central screw.

Another type of variable resistive device is called a *rheostat.* A rheostat is a two-lead variable resistor. Rheostats can be created by simply typing one end of the fixed resistance of a potentiometer to its associated tap. Thus, the potentiometer becomes a two-lead adjustable resistor. Other types of rheostats are available, which are usually intended for high power dissipation. They consist of a fixed wirewound power resistor with a track of the resistive element exposed. An adjustable ring makes contact with this track and is permanently locked at any desired resistance value along the track.

Potentiometers are used specifically in a circuit in which it is necessary to be able to adjust resistance. A typical example is the volume control in a radio circuit. In this case the potentiometer can be designed so that at one end of the track the wiper runs right off the track to break the circuit. Thus the volume control can also be connected up to work as an on-off switch, using this extra facility provided.

Another practical example is the replacement of fixed resistors in a voltage divider by a single potentiometer to make the circuit variable in performance. Thus, the circuit previously described in Fig. 3-7 (Chapter 3) always gives a

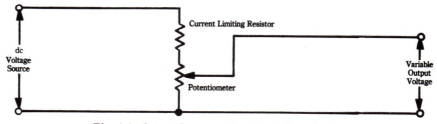

Fig. 4-4. A practical adjustable potential divider.

predetermined voltage at the tapping points (provided the supply voltage remains constant). Replacing resistors R1 and R2 with a potentiometer (Fig. 4-4), with the tapping point taken from one end of the potentiometer and the wiper, will give a tapped voltage that is fully variable from the full supply voltage down to zero, depending on the position of the wiper.

In practice, in a variable-voltage circuit of this type, it may be necessary to leave a fixed resistor in series with the potentiometer to limit the current being drawn in the event that the potentiometer has been adjusted to zero resistance and the tapped circuit is broken or switched off with the original supply still connected. Without the fixed resistor, the supply is shorted. The value of a fixed resistor is calculated to limit the current drawn in such a case to a safe level.

With a fixed resistor in series with the potentiometer, of course, the maximum voltage that can be tapped from the potentiometer is equal to the supply voltage less the voltage dropped by the fixed resistor.

The main thing to watch in such a circuit is that the power rating of the potentiometer is adequate to accommodate the voltage and current drain in the tapped circuit. But it has one further advantage over a fixed resistor potential divider: When a load is added to the tapped circuit, it adds resistance in that circuit, causing a further voltage drop. Unless this is allowed for in calculating the values for the fixed resistors in a potential divider, the load will receive less than the design voltage. With a potentiometer replacing the two fixed resistors, its position can be adjusted to bring the load voltage back to the required figure (Fig. 4.5). This considerably simplifies the design of a potential divider where the load resistance is known only approximately, or not at all.

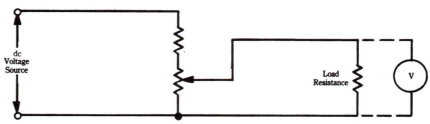

Fig. 4-5. The potentiometer can be adjusted to give required voltage across the load.

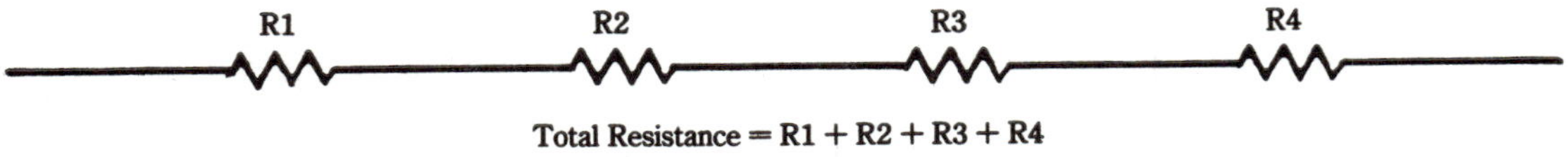

R1   R2   R3   R4

Total Resistance = R1 + R2 + R3 + R4

Fig. 4-6. Resistors in series.

CIRCUIT RULES FOR RESISTORS

In the case of resistances connected in series (Fig. 4-6), the total resistance in circuit will be the sum of the various resistor values; i.e.,

$$\text{total resistance} = R1 + R2 + R3 + \cdots$$

In the case of resistors connected in parallel (Fig. 4-7), the total effective resistance is given by:

$$\frac{1}{R} = \frac{1}{R1} + \frac{1}{R2} + \frac{1}{R3} + \cdots$$

where R is the total resistance.

In the case of two dissimilar resistors:

$$R = \frac{R1 \, R2}{R1 + R2}$$

or remembered as:

$$\text{total resistance} = \frac{\text{product of resistor values}}{\text{sum of resistor values}}$$

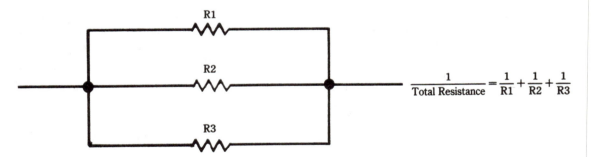

$$\frac{1}{\text{Total Resistance}} = \frac{1}{R1} + \frac{1}{R2} + \frac{1}{R3}$$

Fig. 4-7. Resistors in parallel.

5
Capacitors

A capacitor is basically a device which stores an electric charge. Physically, it consists of two metal plates or electrodes separated by an insulating material or *dielectric*. Application of a dc voltage across the capacitor produces a deficiency of electrons on the positive plate and excess of electrons on the negative plate (Fig. 5-1). This differential accumulation of electrons represents an electrical charge, which builds up a certain level (depending on the voltage) and then remains at that level.

As far as dc is concerned, the insulator acts as a *blocking* device for current flow (although there is a certain transient charging current which stops as soon as the capacitor is fully charged). In the case of ac applied to the capacitor, the charge built up during one half cycle becomes reversed on the second half of the cycle, so that effectively the capacitor conducts current through it as if the dielectric did not exist. Thus, as far as ac is concerned, a capacitor is a coupling device.

There are scarcely any electronic circuits carrying ac which do not incorporate one or more capacitors, either for coupling or shaping the overall frequency response of the network. In the latter case, a capacitor is associated with a resistor to form an *RC* combination (see Chapter 6). The charge/discharge phenomenon associated with capacitors may also be used in other types of circuits (e.g., the photographic electronic flash is operated by the charge and subsequent discharge of a capacitor triggered at the appropriate moment).

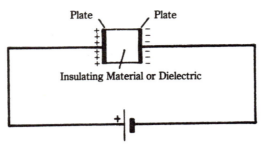

Fig. 5-1. Illustrating how a capacitor builds up a charge when connected to a dc voltage, blocking current flow.

Like resistors, capacitors may be designed to have fixed values or be variable in capacity. Fixed capacitors are the main building blocks of a circuit (together with resistors). Variable capacitors are mainly used for adjusting tuned circuits.

FIXED CAPACITORS

Fixed capacitors fall into two main categories: non-polarized capacitors, and polarized or *electrolytic* capacitors. The main thing which determines the type of capacitor is the dielectric material used.

Non-polarized capacitors consist, basically, of metallic foil interleaves with sheets of solid dielectric material, or equivalent construction. The important thing is that the dielectric is ready made before assembly. As a consequence, it does not matter which plate is made positive or negative. The capacitor works in just the same way, whichever way it is connected in a circuit, hence the description "non-polarized." This is obviously convenient, but this form of construction does limit the amount of capacitance which can be accommodated in a single package of reasonable physical size. Up to about 0.1 microfarads, the package can be made quite small, but for capacitance values much above 1 microfarad, the physical size of a non-polarized capacitor tends to become excessively large in comparison with other components likely to be used in the same circuit.

This limitation does not apply in the case of an electrolytic capacitor. Here, initial construction consists of two electrodes separated by a thin film of *electrolyte*. As a final stage of manufacture, a voltage is applied across the electrodes which has the effect of producing a very thin film of nonconducting metallic oxide on the surface of one plate to form the dielectric. The fact that capacitance of a capacitor increases the thinner the dielectric is made means that very much higher capacitances can be produced in smaller physical sizes. The only disadvantage is that an electrolytic capacitor made in this way will have a polarity corresponding to the original polarity with which the dielectric was formed, this correct polarity being marked on the body of the capacitor. If connected the wrong way in a circuit, the reversed polarity can destroy the dielectric film and permanently ruin the capacitor.

There is also one other characteristic which applies to an electrolytic capacitor. A certain amount of unused electrolyte remains after its initial forming. This acts as a conductor and can make the capacitor quite leaky as far as dc is concerned. This may or may not be acceptable in particular circuits.

NONPOLARIZED CAPACITOR TYPES

Various types of construction are used for nonpolarized capacitors, most of which are easily identified by the shape of the capacitor — see Fig. 5-2. There is no need to go into detail about the actual constructions. Their specific characteristics are important, though, as these can determine the best type to use for a particular application.

Paper Dielectric Capacitors. Generally recognizable by their tubular form, are the lest expensive but generally bulky, value for value, compared with more modern types. Their other main limitation is that they are not suitable for use at frequencies much above 1 MHz, which virtually restricts their application to audio circuits. They are generally available in values from 0.05 μF up to 1 or 2 μF, with working voltages from 200 to 1,000 volts. Plastic-impregnated paper dielectric capacitors may have much higher working voltages.

Ceramic Capacitors. Now widely used in miniaturized audio and rf circuits. They are relatively inexpensive and are available in a wide range of values from 1 pF to 1 μF with high working voltages, and also characterized by high leakage resistance. They are produced in both discs and tubular shapes and as metallized ceramic plates.

Silver-mica Capacitors. More expensive than ceramic capacitors but have excellent high-frequency response and much smaller tolerances, so are generally

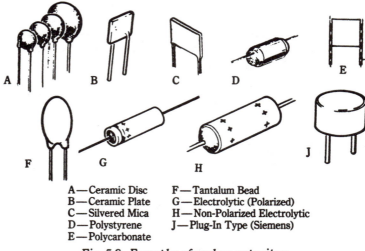

A — Ceramic Disc
B — Ceramic Plate
C — Silvered Mica
D — Polystyrene
E — Polycarbonate
F — Tantalum Bead
G — Electrolytic (Polarized)
H — Non-Polarized Electrolytic
J — Plug-In Type (Siemens)

Fig. 5-2. Examples of modern capacitors.

regarded as superior for critical applications. They can be made with very high working voltages.

Polystyrene Capacitors. Made from metallic foil interleaved with polystyrene film, usually with a fused polystyrene enclosure to ensure high insulation resistance. They are noted for their low losses at high frequencies (i.e., low inductance and low series resistance), good stability and reliability. Values may range from 10 pF to 100,000 pF, but working voltage generally falls substantially with increasing capacitance (e.g., as low as 60 volts for a 100,000 pF polystyrene capacitor).

Polycarbonate Capacitors. Usually produced in the form of rectangular slabs with wire end connections designed to plug into a printed circuit board. They offer high values (up to 1 μF) in very small sizes, with the characteristics of low losses and low inductance. Like polystyrene capacitors, working voltages become more restricted with increasing value.

Polyester Film Capacitors. Also designed for use with printed circuit boards, with values from 0.01 μF up to 2.2 μF. Value for value they are generally larger in physical size than polycarbonate capacitors. Their low inherent inductance makes them particularly suitable for coupling and decoupling applications.

Values of polyester film capacitors are indicated by a color code consisting of five color bands (see Fig. 5-3).

Mylar Film Capacitors. A general-purpose film type, usually available in values from 0.001 μF up to 0.22 μF, with a working voltage up to 100 volts dc.

ELECTROLYTIC CAPACITORS

The original material used for electrolytic capacitors was aluminium foil, together with a paste electrolyte, wound into a tubular form with an aluminum outer cover, characterized by dimpled rings at one or both ends. The modern form of aluminum electrolytic capacitor is based on etched-foil construction, enabling higher capacitance values to be achieved in smaller can sizes. Values available from 1 μF up to 4,700 μF (or even larger, if required). Working voltages are generally low, but may range from 10 volts up to 250 or 500 volts dc,

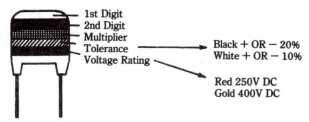

Fig. 5-3. Color code for polyester capacitors.

| | Capacitance in μF | | | 3rd Ring dc | Working Voltage |
COLOR	1st Ring	2nd Ring	Spot Polarity and Multiplier	Color	Voltage
Black	—	0	×1.00	White	3
Brown	1	1	×	Yellow	6.3
Red	2	2		Black	10
Orange	3	3		Green	16
Yellow	4	4		Grey	25
Green	5	5		Pink	35
Blue	6	6			
Violet	7	7			
Grey	8	8	×0.01		
White	9	9	×0.10		

Fig. 5-4. Color code for tantalum bead capacitors.

depending on value and construction. A single lead emerges from each end, but single-ended types (both leads emerging from one end), and can-types with rigid leads in one end for plugging into a socket are also available. Single-ended types are preferred for mounting on printed-circuit boards.

The other main types of electrolytic is the *tantalum capacitor.* This is produced both in cylindrical configuration with axial leads, or in *tantalum-bead* configuration. Both (and the latter type particularly) can offer very high capacitance values in small physical sizes, within the range 0.1 to 100 μF. Voltage ratings are generally low; from 35 volts down to less than 10 volts dc.

All electrolytic capacitors normally have their value marked on the body or case, together with a polarity marking (+ indicating the positive lead). Tantalum-bead capacitors, however, are sometimes color coded instead of marked with values. This color coding is shown in Fig. 5-4, while other codes which may be found on other types of non-polarized capacitors are given in Fig. 5-5.

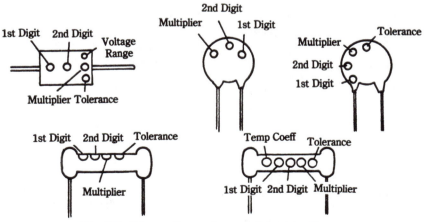

Fig. 5-5. Other coding systems used on capacitors.

Tolerance of Fixed Capacitors

As a general rule, only silver-mica capacitors are made to close tolerances (plus or minus 1 percent is usual). The tolerance on other types of capacitors is usually between 10 and 20 percent and may be even higher (as much as 50 percent) in the case of aluminum foil electrolytics. Because of the wide tolerances normal with electrolytics, choice of actual value is seldom critical.

VARIABLE CAPACITORS

Variable capacitors are based on interleaved sets of metal plates, one set being fixed and the other movable. The plates are separated by a dielectric which may be air or a solid dielectric. Movement of one set of plates alters the effective area of the plates, and thus the value of capacitance present.

There is also a general distinction between *tuning capacitors* used for frequent adjustment (e.g., to tune a radio receiver to a particular station) and *trimmer capacitors* used for initial adjustment of a tuned circuit. Tuning capacitors are larger, more robust in construction and generally of air-dielectric type. Trimmer capacitors are usually based on a mica or film dielectric with a smaller number of plates, capacitance being adjusted by turning a central screw to vary the pressure between plates and mica. Because they are smaller in size, however, a trimmer capacitor may sometimes be used as a tuning capacitor on a sub-miniature radio circuit, although special miniature tuning capacitors are made, designed to mount directly on a printed-circuit board.

In the case of tuning capacitors, the shape of the vanes determines the manner in which capacitance changes with spindle movement. These characteristics usually fall under one of the following descriptions:

- *Linear*—where each degree of spindle rotation produces an equal change in capacitance. This is the most usual type chosen for radio receivers.
- *Logarithmic*—where each degree of spindle movement produces a constant *percentage* change in *frequency* of a tuned circuit.
- *Even frequency*—where each degree of spindle movement produces an *equal* change in frequency in a tuned circuit.
- *Square law*—where the change in capacitance is proportional to the *square* of the angle of spindle movement.

BASIC CIRCUIT RULES FOR CAPACITORS

The rules for total capacitance of capacitors in series and in parallel are opposite to that for resistors. For capacitors connected in *series* (Fig. 5-6), the total effective capacitance (C) is given by:

$$\frac{1}{\text{Total Capacitance}} = \frac{1}{C1} + \frac{1}{C2} + \frac{1}{C3}$$

Fig. 5-6. Capacitors in series.

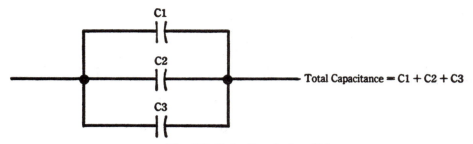

Fig. 5-7. Capacitors in parallel.

$$\frac{1}{C} = \frac{1}{C1} + \frac{1}{C2} + \frac{1}{C3} + \cdots$$

or, in the case of two dissimilar capacitors

$$C = \frac{C1\ C2}{C1 + C2}$$

In words:

$$\text{total capacitance} = \frac{\text{product of capacitances}}{\text{sum of capacitances}}$$

For capacitors connected in parallel (Fig. 5-7):

$$C = C1 + C2 + C3 + \cdots$$

This capacitance effect, of course, is only apparent in an ac circuit. In a dc circuit a capacitor simply builds up a charge without passing current. In a practical ac circuit, a capacitor also exhibits *reactance* (see Chapter 2), and because of its construction, may also exhibit a certain amount of *inductance* (see Chapter 7).

6
Capacitor and RC Circuits

One of the principal uses of a capacitor is as a coupling device capable of passing ac but acting as a block to dc. In any practical circuit, there will be some resistance connected in series with the capacitor (e.g., the resistive load of the circuit being coupled), This resistance limits the current flow and leads to a certain delay between the application of a voltage to the capacitor and the build-up of charge on the capacitor equivalent to that voltage. It is this charge voltage which blocks the passage of dc. At the same time, the combination of resistance with capacitance, generally abbreviated to RC, acts as a *filter* capable of passing ac frequencies, depending on the charge-discharge time of the capacitor, or the *time constant* of the RC combination.

TIME CONSTANT

The formula for calculating the time constant (t) is quite simple:

$$t = RC$$

where:

t = time constant in seconds
R = resistance in ohms
C = capacitance in farads

(It can be noted that the same numerical value for T is given if R is in ohms and C in farads, but megohms and microfarads are usually much more convenient units.)

The time constant is actually the time for the voltage across the capacitor in an RC combination to reach 63 percent of the applied voltage (this 63 percent figure is chosen as a mathematical convenience). The voltage across the capacitor goes on building up to almost (but never quite) 100 percent of the applied voltage, as shown in Fig. 6-1.

The *time-constant factor* refers to the duration of time in terms of the time factor; e.g., at 1 (which *is* the time factor of the RC combinations) 63 percent full voltage has been built up, in a time equal to 2 times the time constant, 80 percent full voltage; and so on. After a time constant of 5 the full (almost 100 percent) voltage has been built up across the capacitor.

The discharge characteristics of a capacitor take place in essentially the inverse manner; e.g., after a period of time equal to the time constant the voltage across the capacitor has dropped 100 − 63 = 37 percent of the full voltage and so on.

In theory, at least, a capacitor never charges up to full applied voltage; nor does it fully discharge. In practice, full charge, or complete discharge, can be considered as being achieved in a period of time equal to five time constants. Thus, in the circuit identified with Fig. 6-2, closing switch 1 produces a full charge on the capacitor in 5 times time constant seconds. If switch 1 is now opened, the capacitor then remains in a condition of storing a voltage equivalent to the original applied voltage, holding this charge indefinitely if there is no internal leakage. In practice, it very slowly loses its charge, as no practical capacitor is perfect, but for some considerable time it remains effectively as a potential source of full-charge voltage. If the capacitor is part of a high-voltage circuit, for example, it is readily capable of giving an electric shock if touched for some time after the circuit has been switched off.

To complete the cycle of charge-discharge as shown in the second diagram of Fig. 6-1, switch 2 is closed, when the capacitor discharges through the associated resistance, taking a finite amount of time to complete its discharge.

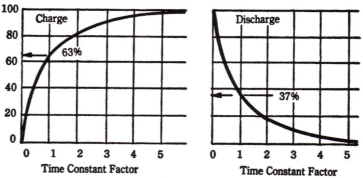

Fig. 6-1. Percentage voltage across capacitor related to time when being charged (left) and discharge (right).

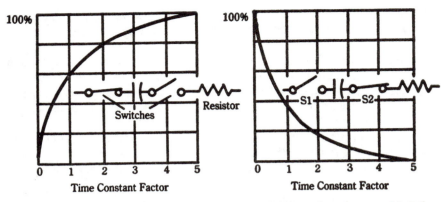

Time Constant Factor   Time Constant Factor

Fig. 6-2. Closing switch 1 allows capacitor to charge right up in a time equal to 5 time constants. It then takes a similar period to discharge fully through a load resistor when switch 2 is closed.

Figure 6-3 shows a very simple circuit that works on this principle. It consists of a resistor (R) and capacitor (C) connected in series to a source of dc voltage. As a visual indication of the working of the circuit, a neon lamp is connected in parallel with the capacitor. The lamp represents a virtually open circuit until its threshold voltage is applied, when it immediately conducts current like a low resistance and glows (see Chapter 10 for more about neons). The voltage source for this current must therefore be above that of the neon turn-on voltage.

When this circuit is switched on, the capacitor starts to build up a charge at a rate depending on the time constant of R and C. The lamp is fed by voltage developed across the capacitor. Once this reaches the turn-on voltage of the lamp, the lamp switches on and causes the capacitor to discharge through the neon gas, causing it to glow. Once the capacitor has discharged, no more current flows through the lamp and so it switches off again until the capacitor has built up another charge equivalent to the turn-on voltage, when it discharges through the lamp, and so on. In other words, the neon lamp will flash at a rate determined by the time constant of R and C.

Using the component values shown, the time constant for the circuit is:

$$t = 5 \text{ (megohms)} \times 0.1 \text{ (microfarads)}$$
$$= 0.5 \text{ seconds}$$

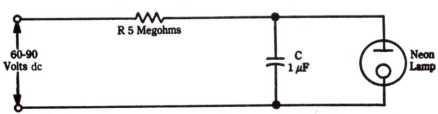

Fig. 6-3. Simple neon flasher circuit (note the symbol for a neon lamp). The values of the resistor (R) and capacitor (C) determine the flashing rate.

This is not necessarily the actual flashing rate of the circuit. It may take a period of more than one time constant (or less) for the capacitor voltage to build up to the neon turn-on voltage—more if the turn-on voltage is greater than 63 percent of the supply voltage; less if the turn-on voltage is less than 63 percent of the supply voltage.

It also follows that the flashing rate can be altered by altering the value of R or C, either by substituting different values calculated to give a different time constant, or with a parallel-connected resistor or capacitor. Connecting a similar value resistor in parallel with R, for example, would double the flashing rate (since paralleling similar resistor values halves the total resistance). Connecting a similar value capacitor in parallel with C halves the flashing rate.

This type of circuit is known as a *relaxation oscillator.* Using a variable resistor for R it can be adjusted for a specific flashing rate. It can also be extended in the form of a novelty lighting system by connecting a series of RC circuits, each with a neon lamp in cascade, each RC combination with a different time constant —Fig. 6-4. This produces random flashing of the neons in the complete circuit.

CAPACITORS IN AC CIRCUITS

As far as ac is concerned, the fact that the applied voltage is alternating means that during one half cycle the capacitor is effectively being charged and discharged with one direction of voltage; and during the second half of the ac cycle, charged and discharged with opposite direction of voltage. Thus, in effect, ac voltages pass through the capacitor, restricted only by such limitations as may be applied by the RC time constant which determines what proportion of the applied voltage is built up and discharged through the capacitor. At the same time, the capacitor offers a certain opposition to the passage of ac through reactance (see Chapter 3), although this does not actually consume power. Its main influence is on frequency response of RC circuits.

SIMPLE COUPLING

Coupling one stage of a radio receiver to the next stage via a capacitor is common design practice. Although the capacitance is apparently used on its own, it is associated with an effective series resistance represented by the load of the

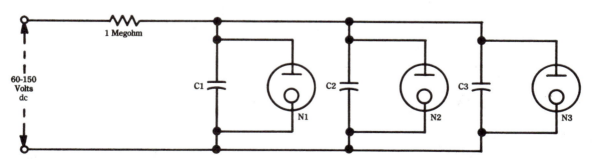

Fig. 6-4. Random cascade flasher circuit. Any number of lamps can be connected in this way and will flash in random order.

stage being fed—Fig. 6-5. This, together with the capacitor, forms an RC combination which has a particular time constant. It is important that this time constant matches the requirements of the ac signal *frequency* being passed from one stage to the other.

In the case of AM radio stage, the maximum signal likely to be present is 10 kHz. The cycle time of such a signal is 1/10,000 = 0.1 milliseconds. However, to pass this frequency each cycle represents two charge/discharge functions as far as the coupling capacitor is concerned, one positive and one negative. Thus the time period for a single charge/discharge function is 0.05 milliseconds.

The RC time constant necessary to accommodate this application must be a value capable of passing 63 percent of the applied ac voltage—and preferably more than 63 percent of the applied voltage.

These figures can give you a clue as to the optimum value of the coupling capacitor to use. For example, the typical input resistance of a low power transistor is of the order of 1,000 ohms. The time constant of a matching RC coupling would be 0.05 milliseconds (see above), giving the requirements:

$$t = RC \therefore C = \frac{t}{R}$$
$$= \frac{0.05 \times 10^{-3}}{1 \times 10^3}$$
$$= 0.05 \times 10^{-6}$$
$$= 0.05 \ \mu F$$

(or higher, since this would ensure more than 63 percent voltage passed).

In practice, a much higher capacitance value would normally be used; even as high as 1 μF or more. This usually gives better results, at the expense of efficiency of ac (in this case rf) transmission. (An apparent contradiction, but it happens to work out that way because the load is *reactive* rather than purely resistive.) What the simple calculation does show is that capacitive coupling becomes increasingly less efficient with decreasing frequency of ac signal when associated with practical values of capacitors used for coupling duties.

FILTER CIRCUITS

A basic RC combination used as a *filter circuit* is shown in Fig. 6-6. From the input side, this represents a resistor in series with a capacitive *reactance*, with a

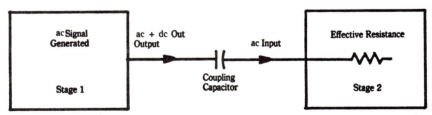

Fig. 6-5. Basic function of a coupling capacitor is to pass ac signals and block dc signals. It also passes undulating dc signals.

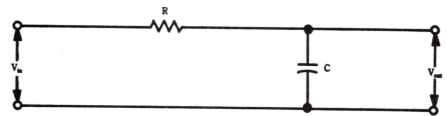

Fig. 6-6. *Basic filter circuit. It blocks ac frequencies higher than the cutoff frequency of the combination of R and C.*

voltage drop across each component. If the reactance of the capacitor (X_C) is much greater than R, most of the input voltage appears across the capacitor and thus the output voltage approaches the input voltage in value. Reactance is inversely proportional to frequency, however, and so with increasing frequency the reactance of the capacitor decreases, and so does the output voltage (an increasing proportion of the input voltage being dropped by the resistor).

As far as effective passage of ac is concerned, there is a critical frequency at which the reactance component becomes so degraded in value that such a circuit starts to become blocking rather than conductive; i.e., the ratio of volts$_{out}$/volts$_{in}$ starts to fall rapidly. This is shown in simplified diagrammatic form in Fig. 6-7. The critical point, known as the roll-off point or *cutoff frequency* (f_c), is given by:

$$f_c = \frac{1}{2\pi\,RC}$$

where:

R is in ohms
C is in farads
$\pi = 3.1416$

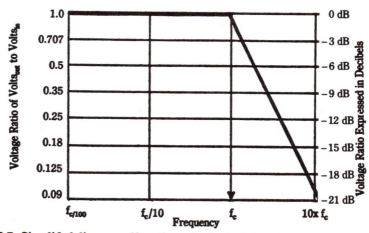

Fig. 6-7. *Simplified diagram of how the ratio of volts in/volts out drops rapidly as the cutoff frequency of a filter is exceeded. All signals below the cutoff frequency are passed without attenuation.*

But RC, as noted previously, is equal to the time constant of the RC combination. Hence:

$$f_c = \frac{1}{2\pi\,T}$$

where T is the time constant, in seconds.

The performance of such a filter is defined by its cutoff frequency and the rate at which the volts$_{in}$/volts$_{out}$ ratio falls above the cutoff frequency. The latter is normally quoted as (so many) dB per octave (or each doubling of frequency) (see Fig. 6-8) which shows the relationship between dB and volts$_{in}$/volts$_{out}$ ratio, and also the true form of the frequency response curve.

LOW-PASS FILTERS

Circuits of this type are called *low-pass filters* because they pass ac signals below the cut-off frequency with little or no loss or *attenuation* of signal strength. With signals above the cutoff frequency, there is increasing attenuation. Suitable component values are readily calculated. For example, a typical *scratch filter* associated with a record player or amplifier would be designed to attenuate frequencies above, say, 10 kHz—Fig. 6-9. This value represents the cutoff frequency required; i.e., Any combination of R (in ohms) and C (in farads) giving this product value could be used.

HIGH-PASS FILTERS

High-pass filters work the other way around. They attenuate frequencies below the cutoff frequency, but pass frequencies at and above the cut-off fre-

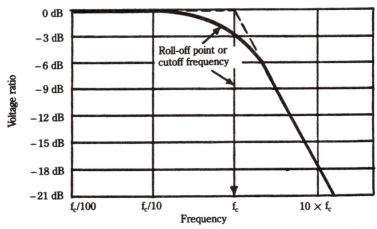

Fig. 6-8. The actual roll-off point on the frequency response curve of a filter is not sharply defined. The cutoff frequency is really a nominal figure and generally taken as the frequency at which there is a 3 decibel loss or a volts in/volts out ratio of 0.707. This is equivalent to a 50 percent loss of power.

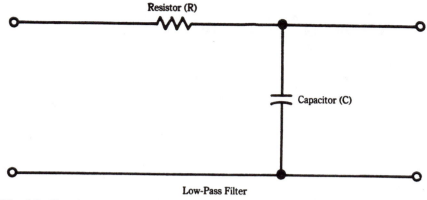

Fig. 6-9. Simple scratch filter circuit. Any combination of component values giving a product of RC = 1600 will work.

quency with no attenuation. To achieve this mode of working, the two components in the circuit are interchanged (Fig. 6-10).

This type of filter is again commonly associated with record player circuits, incorporated to eliminate low-frequency noise or "rumble" which may be present. The design cutoff frequency must be low enough not to interfere with bass response, and so the value chosen is usually of the order of 15 to 20 Hz. Exactly the same formula is used to determine the cutoff frequency, hence, using a design value of 20 Hz:

$$20 = \frac{1}{2\pi \, RC}$$

$$RC = 125$$

Again, any combination of R (in ohms) and C (in farads) giving a product of 125 would work.

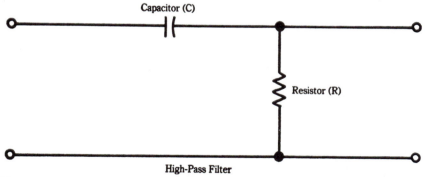

Fig. 6-10. (Right) High-pass or rumble filters cut off low frequencies but pass high frequencies. A typical value for the product RC in this case would be 125.

In practical circuits, such filters are normally inserted in the preamplifier stage, or in the amplifier immediately in front of the tone control circuit. For hi-fi systems, the type of filter circuits used are considerably more complicated than the ones described.

For more advanced filter designs, see the appendix.

7
Coils and Inductances

The flow of electric current through any conductor has the effect of generating a magnetic field. This creation of magnetic energy represents a power loss during the time that field is being created, which is measurable in terms of a voltage drop or *back emf*. This is quite different (and additional) to the voltage drop produced by the resistance of the conductor, and disappears once stable conditions have been reached. Thus, in a dc circuit, the back emf tends to prevent the current rising rapidly when the circuit is switched on. Once a constant magnetic field has been established, the back emf disappears since no further energy is being extracted from the circuit and transferred to the magnetic field.

In the case of an ac circuit, the current is continually changing, creating a back emf which is also changing at a similar rate. The value of the back emf is dependent both on the rate of change of current (frequency) and to a factor dependent on the form of the conductor which governs its *inductance*. Inductance is thus another form of resistance to ac, generated in addition to the pure resistance.

Every conductor has inductance when carrying ac, although in the case of straight wires this is usually negligible (except at very high frequencies). If the wire is wound in the form of a coil, however, its inductance is greatly increased. If the coil is fitted with an iron core, then its inductance is even higher for the same number of turns and coil size.

With the ac flowing through the coil, the "resistive" condition established is not as drastic as may appear at first sight. The polarity of the back emf is always such as to oppose any change in current. Thus while the current is increasing, work is being done against the back emf by storing energy in the magnetic field. On the next part of the current cycle when the current is falling, the stored energy in the magnetic field returns to the circuit, thus tending to keep the current flowing (see Fig. 7-1). An inductance, in fact, may be a very good conductor of ac, especially when combined with a capacitor in a *tuned circuit* (see later). On the other hand, it may be designed to work as a resistive component or *choke*.

The inductance of a single-layer coil, wound with space between adjacent turns can be calculated from the formula:

$$L = \frac{R^2 N^2}{9R + 10L}$$

where:

L is the inductance in microhenrys
R is the radius of the coil in inches
N is the number of turns
L is the length of the coil in inches.

Written as a solution for the number of turns required to produce a given inductance with R and L predetermined:

$$N = \sqrt{\frac{(9R + 10L) \times L}{R^2}}$$

This formula applies regardless of the actual diameter of the wire used (also, it does not matter whether bare wire or insulated wire is used), provided the coil diameter is much larger than the wire diameter. For practical sizes of wires used for coil winding, this means a minimum coil diameter of at least 1 inch (25 mm).

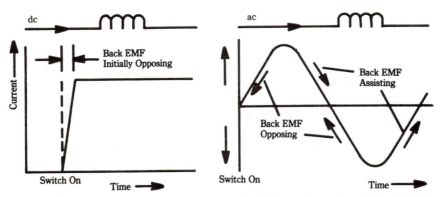

Fig. 7-1. Back emf induced in a dc circuit on switching on exists only momentarily. In an ac circuit, the back emf is continually changing.

For smaller diameter coils, the wire size has an increasing modifying effect on the actual inductance, and even the length of leads at the ends of the coil can upset the calculation. Thus such coils are normally designed on empirical lines (i.e., based on a specified number of turns of a given size of wire known to produce a given inductance when wound on a specific form diameter).

In practice, small coils are normally wound on a form intended to take an iron core. The position of this core is adjustable, relative to the wound coil, by screwing in or out. Thus the actual value of inductance can be varied for tuning purposes (Fig. 7-2, left).

Alternatively a *pot core* may be used where the coil is wound on a form or bobbin, subsequently enclosed in an iron housing. Provided the *specific inductance* of the pot core is known (it is usually specified by the manufacturer), the number of turns (μ) to be used for the winding can be calculated with good accuracy from the formula:

$$N = \sqrt{\frac{L}{A_L}}$$

where L is the inductance required, and A_L is the quoted specific inductance of the pot core in the same units as L.

Practical values of inductance used in electronic circuits may range from microhenrys (in medium and high frequency circuits) to millihenrys (in low frequency circuits), up to several henrys for chokes in power supply circuits. Normally, an inductance will be wound from the largest diameter enameled wire it is convenient to use (and still get the required number of turns on the form or bobbin), because this will minimize ohmic resistance and thus improve the efficiency or *Q-factor* of the coil.

RESONANT CIRCUITS

A coil (inductance) and a capacitor connected in series across an ac supply has the very important characteristic that it is possible for the reactive effect of one to cancel out the reactive effects of the other. Thus in the demonstration circuit shown in Fig. 7-3, L is the inductance, and C the capacitor connected across a source of ac, the frequency of which can be varied. A resistor (R) is shown in series with L and C, as an inevitable part of a practical circuit.

If the ac supply is adjusted to a low frequency, the capacitive reactance will be very much larger than R, and the inductive reactance will be much lower than R

Fig. 7-2. Coil form (left) and pot cores (right).

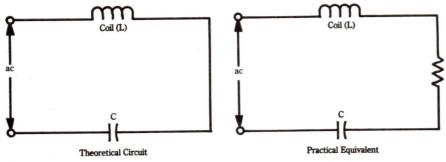

Fig. 7-3. *Components which make a resonant circuit.*

(and thus also very much lower than the capacitive reactance). See Chapter 3 for the formulas for capacitive and inductive reactance, and how these values are dependent on frequency.

If the ac supply is adjusted to a high frequency the opposite conditions will apply — inductive reactance much larger than R, and capacitive reactance lower than R and L. Somewhere between these two extremes there is an ac frequency at which the reactances of the capacitance and inductance are equal, and this is the really interesting point. When inductive reactance (X_L) equals capacitive reactance (X_C), the voltage drops across these two components will be equal but *180 degrees out of phase.* This means the two voltage drops cancel each other out, with the result that only R is effective as total resistance to current flow. In other words, maximum current flows through the circuit, determined only by the value of R and the applied ac voltage.

Working under these conditions, the circuit is said to be *resonant.* Obviously, resonance occurs only at a specific frequency, which is thus called the *resonant frequency.* Its value is given by the simple formula:

$$f = \frac{1}{2\pi \sqrt{LC}}$$

where:

f = resonant frequency in Hz
L = inductance in henrys
C = capacitance in farads.

A more convenient formula to use is:

$$f = \frac{10^6}{2\pi \sqrt{LC}}$$

where:

f = resonant frequency in kilohertz (kHz)

$$L = \text{inductance in microhenrys } (\mu H)$$
$$C = \text{capacitance in pico farads (pF).}$$

Note that the formula for resonant frequency is not affected by any resistance (R) in the circuit. The presence of resistance does, however, affect the Quality factor or Q of the circuit. This is a measure of how *sharply* the circuit can be tuned to resonance, the higher the value of Q the better, in this respect. The actual value of Q is given by:

$$Q = \frac{X}{R}$$

where X is the reactance in ohms of either the inductance or capacitance at the resonant frequency (they are both the same, so it does not matter which one is taken) and R is the value of the series resistance in ohms.

The practical resonant circuit (or tuned circuit) is based on just two components — an inductance and a capacitor. Some resistance is always present, however. At low to moderately high frequencies, most of this resistance comes from the wire from which the coil is wound. At very much higher frequencies, the majority of the resistance may come from the frequency energy loss in the capacitor.

TUNED CIRCUITS

The combination of an inductance and capacitance in series is the standard form of *tuned circuit* used in almost every radio receiver. Figure 7-4 illustrates a tuned circuit with the inductor and capacitor in a parallel configuration. The impedance (Z) of this circuit is opposite in effect to the circuit shown in Fig. 7-3. As previously discussed, when the resonant frequency is applied to the circuit shown in Fig. 7-3, the circuit current is at its highest (meaning its impedance is at minimum). The circuit illustrated in Fig. 7-4 presents its highest impedance at its point of resonance.

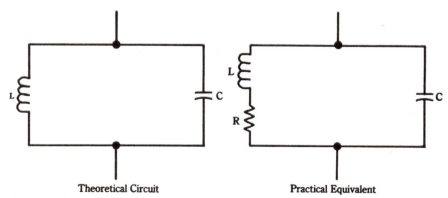

Theoretical Circuit   Practical Equivalent

Fig. 7-4. Theoretically, only a capacitor and inductance are involved in a resonant circuit. In practice, some resistance is always present as well.

To make the circuit tunable over a range of resonant frequencies, either component can be a variable type. The usual choice for antenna circuits is to make the capacitor variable. In practice, the coil may also have variable characteristics. It is usually wound on a sleeve fitted on a ferrite rod, and capable of being moved up and down the rod, providing a means of varying the effective inductance. Once an optimum position has been found for the coil, it is cemented to the rod. In other words, the variable characteristics of the coil are used only for initial adjustment. After that, all adjustment of resonant frequency, or tuning, is done by the variable capacitor.

To assist in selecting suitable component values, the resonant frequency formula can be rewritten:

$$LC = \frac{10^{12}}{4\pi^2 f^2}$$

where L is in microhenrys, C is in picofarads, and f is the frequency in kHz.

Maximum values of variable capacitor used are normally 300 pF or 500 pF. The working formula for calculating a matching inductance value is:

$$L(\text{microhenrys}) = \frac{10^{12}}{4\pi^2 f^2 C}$$

As an example, suppose the tuned circuit is to be designed to cover the medium waveband, or frequencies from 500 to 1,600 kHz; and a 500 pF tuning capacitor is to be used. It follows from the resonant frequency formula that maximum capacitance will correspond to the lowest resonant frequency (with a fixed inductance), which in this case is 500 kHz. Inserting these values in the working formula:

$$L(\text{microhenrys}) = \frac{10^{12}}{4\pi^2 \times (500)^2 \times 500}$$

$$= 200$$

Now check the *resonant frequency* when the capacitor is turned to its minimum value (which will probably be about 50 pF, associated with this value of inductance:

$$f = \sqrt{\frac{10^{12}}{4\pi^2 LC}}$$

$$= \sqrt{\frac{10^{12}}{4\pi^2 \times 200 \times 50}} = 1,600 \text{ kHz}$$

This shows that a 50–500 pF variable capacitor will tune the circuit from

Fig. 7-5. A series-resonant circuit. The impedance across the terminals of the circuit is very low at the frequency of resonance; at the connection between the capacitor and inductor, the impedance is very high. The capacitor is usually the variable element in this arrangement.

1500 kHz (the highest frequency), down to 500 kHz satisfactorily. In other words, it covers the whole of the medium wave broadcast band.

If the final results achieved in the circuit do not provide quite the coverage required (for example, a station near one end of the band is not picked up) then there is still the possibility of shifting the frequency coverage in one direction or the other by adjusting the inductance (i.e., sliding the coil up or down the ferrite rod).

There are other type of tuned circuits which normally require adjustment only when initially setting up. These normally employ a tunable inductance (e.g., a coil wound on a form with an adjustable powdered-iron core). Such circuits may also be tuned by a trimmer capacitor, or both a trimmer capacitor and tunable inductance. The latter combination provides double tuning.

SERIES-RESONANT CIRCUITS

Another arrangement of the coil-capacitor combination is to connect them in series (Fig. 7-5). This produces a *series-resonant* circuit wherein the reactances of the coil and capacitor are again equal but opposite. The difference is that it presents a low impedance at the terminals of the circuit (top and bottom). This low impedance has the effect of shunting the ac frequency of resonance out of the circuit. Frequencies other than the resonant one are not affected by the tuned circuit, as the off-resonance impedance is undisturbed.

A common use for this type of circuit is to remove, or reduce in amplitude, any unwanted signals, while allowing all others to pass. A popular application of the series-resonant circuit is in the antenna or rf-amplifier stages of receivers, where it is often called a *wave-trap*. It can also be used quite effectively in transmitter power-amplifier stages to trap unwanted multiples (harmonics) of the fundamental frequency of operation.

RADIO-FREQUENCY CHOKES

A radio frequency choke (*rfc*) is a coil or inductance so designed that it has a relatively low ohmic resistance but a very high reactance at radio frequencies. It

Fig. 7-6. Typical appearance of chokes wound on a ferrite core.

can thus pass dc but blocks high frequency ac when the two are present in the same circuit (Fig. 7-6). In other words, it really works the opposite to a capacitor as a circuit element in this respect.

The characteristics of any rfc vary with frequency. At high frequencies it has characteristics similar to that of a parallel-resonant circuit; and at low frequencies characteristics similar to that of a series-resonant circuit. At intermediate frequencies, it has intermediate characteristics. The actual characteristics are relatively unimportant when an rfc is used for series feed because the rf voltage across the choke is negligible. If used for parallel feed (where the choke is shunted across a tank circuit), it must have sufficiently high impedance at the lowest frequencies and no series-resonance characteristics at the higher frequencies in order to reduce power absorption to a suitable level. Otherwise, there is a danger of the choke being overloaded and burned out.

Chokes designed to maintain at least a critical value of inductance over the likely range of current likely to flow through them are called *swinging chokes.* They are used as input filters on power supplies to reduce *ripple,* or residual ac content. Chokes designed specifically for smoothing ripple, and having a substantially constant inductance, independent of changes in current, are known as *smoothing chokes.*

8
Transformers

A transformer consists of two coils so positioned that they have mutual inductance. This magnetic coupling effect can be further enhanced by winding the two coils on a common iron core (see Fig. 8-1). The coil which is connected to the source of supply is called the *primary,* and the other coil is called the *secondary.* In order to transfer electrical energy from primary to secondary, the magnetic field must be continually changing; i.e., the supply must be ac.

One of the most useful characteristics of a transformer is its ability to step-down (or step-up) ac voltages. The step-down (or step-up) ratio is proportional to the number of turns in each coil:

$$V_s = N_s/N_p \times V_p$$

where:

V_s = secondary voltage
N_s = number of turns on secondary
N_p = number of turns on primary
V_p = primary voltage.

The currents flowing in the primary and secondary follow a similar relationship, but in opposite ratio:

$$I_s = N_p/N_s \times I_p$$

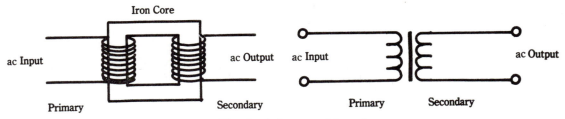

Fig. 8-1. The simple iron-cored transformer.

where:

I_s = secondary current
I_p = primary current

In other words, a step-down in voltage produces a step-up in current, and vice versa.

In practice, there are always some losses due to the resistance of the coils and energy lost in hysteresis and eddy currents in the core (in the case of an iron-cored transformer), and also from reactance caused by a leak of inductance from both coils. Thus, the power which can be taken from the secondary is always less than the power put into the primary, the ratio of the two powers being a measure of the *efficiency* of the transformer.

Typically, efficiency may range from 60 percent upwards, but is not necessarily constant. A transformer is usually designed to have its maximum efficiency at its rated power output. Its actual efficiency figure decreases if the output is higher or lower. This loss of power appears in the form of heat. Thus, overloading a transformer can both reduce its efficiency and increase the heating effect. Operating at reduced output has no harmful effect, except for reducing efficiency because the actual power loss (and thus heating effect) is lowered.

TRANSFORMERS AS POWER SUPPLIES

By selecting a suitable turns ratio, a transformer can be used directly to convert an ac supply voltage into a lower (or higher) ac output voltage at efficiencies which may be as high as 90 percent (Fig. 8-2). There are also applications where a 1 : 1 turns ratio transformer is used, providing the same ac output voltage as the ac input voltage, where it is desirable to isolate the supply from the output circuit. All transformers do, of course, provide physical separation of input and output circuits, but the degree of isolation safety is very much dependent on the actual construction of the transformer.

The more usual power-supply application of a transformer is to step-down an ac voltage into some lower dc voltage output. The transformer only provides voltage conversion. Additional components are needed in the output circuit to transform the converted ac voltage into a dc voltage.

Two basic circuits for doing this are shown in Fig. 8-3. The first uses a single diode and provides *half-wave rectification,* passing one half of each ac cycle as dc

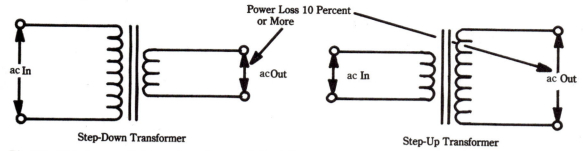

Fig. 8-2. Step-down and step-up transformers defined. In practice, transformers are often drawn in symbolic form with both coils of the same length, regardless of actual turns ratio.

and suppressing the other half cycle. The purpose of the capacitor is to maintain the dc voltage output as far as possible by discharging on each suppressed half cycle, and for this a large value capacitor is required. Although a very simple circuit, it has the inherent disadvantage of generating high *peak* voltages and currents, especially if a high current is drawn from the output. Also, the dc output is far from smooth. It has a ripple at the ac frequency.

Much can be done to smooth the output by adding an inductance or choke and a second capacitor, as shown in the second diagram. These two components work as a filter (see also Chapter 6). The design of the choke has to be specially matched to the requirements, offering low resistance to dc without becoming saturated, which could reduce its inductance. In particular circuits the inductance may be a swinging choke, when it is possible to eliminate the reservoir capacitor C1.

The first diagram of Fig. 8-4 shows a simple *full-wave rectifier* circuit added to the transformer (the secondary of which must be center tapped). For the same secondary voltage as the half-wave rectifier, the dc output voltage is now halved, but the current which can be drawn for a given rectifier rating is doubled. The reservoir capacitor charges and discharges alternately. This produces a smoother dc supply, but ripple is still present and in this case is equal to twice the ac frequency.

The more usual form of full-wave rectifier is the *bridge circuit,* shown in the second diagram of Fig. 8-4. This gives approximately the same no-load voltage as a half-wave rectifier with the advantage of full-wave rectification and better smoothing.

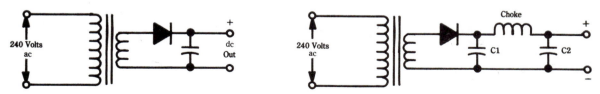

Fig. 8-3. Half-wave rectification of ac.

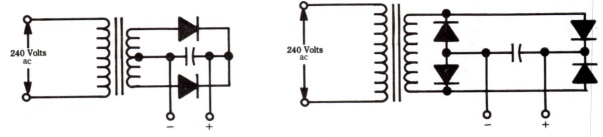

Fig. 8-4. Full-wave rectification of ac.

A practical circuit of this type is shown in Fig. 8-5. A single high value electrolytic capacitor is used for smoothing. Additional smoothing between stages fed from such a power supply may be provided by a resistor, associated with a decoupling capacitor (like Fig. 8-3). The resistor value can also be chosen to drop a specific amount of voltage if the previous stage(s) do not require the full power-supply output voltage.

TRANSFORMERS AS COUPLING DEVICES

Transformers are very useful coupling elements for ac circuits. As well as providing coupling they can step-up a voltage or current, and even more important for *impedance matching*. By choosing the proper turns ratio, the impedance of a fixed load can be transformed to any desired higher or lower impedance, within practical limits. This can be a particularly important requirement when coupling transistor radio stages.

For impedance matching, the following relationship applies:

$$\frac{N_p}{N_s} = \sqrt{\frac{Z_p}{Z_s}}$$

where:

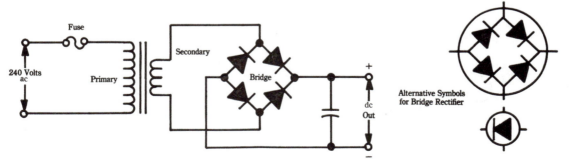

Fig. 8-5. Practical power-supply circuit. A high value capacitor is used. The four diodes are bought as a single component called a bridge rectifier.

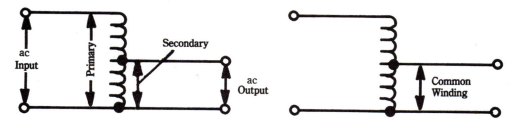

Fig. 8-6. The autotransformer is a single full-length coil with a tapping point.

Z_p is the impedance of the transformer looking into the primary terminals

Z_s is the impedance of the load connected to the secondary of the transformer

For impedance matching, it is therefore necessary to design the primary to provide the required Z_p and select the turns ratio to satisfy the equation.

AUTOTRANSFORMERS

An *autotransformer* is a one-winding coil with an intermediate tapping point. The full length of the coil (usually) forms the primary, and the length of coil between the tapping point and one end of the coil serves as the secondary (Fig. 8-6). It works on exactly the same principle as a conventional transformer, with the voltage developed across the output proportional to the turns ratio of this length of coil to the full length of coil. The biggest disadvantage of an autotransformer is that it does not provide isolation between the primary and secondary windings. This can be critical (or even dangerous) in some high-power applications.

9
Semiconductors

Resistors, capacitors and inductances are known as *passive* components. Devices which produce changes in circuit conditions by reacting to applied signals are known as *active* components. The majority of active components used in modern electronic circuits are *semiconductors,* or more correctly put, devices based on semiconductor materials.

Very simply, a semiconductor material is one which can be given a predominance of mobile negative charges or electrons, or positive charges or *holes.* Current can flow through the material from the movement of both electrons and holes. This is quite different from the behavior of a normal conductor, where current flow is the result of electrons *through* the material (see Chapter 1).

Semiconductor properties can be given to a strictly limited number of materials by doping with minute traces of impurities. The two main semiconductor materials are germanium and silicon (both non-metals or "semi metals"). Doping can produce a material with either a predominance of *P*ositive charges (holes) resulting in a *P-type* material; or with a predominance of *N*egative charges (electrons), known as an *N-type* material.

This does not become particularly significant until a single crystal (of germanium or silicon) is treated with both a P-type dope and an N-type dope. In this case, two separate regions are formed — a P-region and an N-region. Since these regions have opposite charges there is a tendency for electrons to mirate from the N-zone to the P-zone, and holes to migrate from the P-zone into the N-zone. The effect is a cancellation of charges in the region of the junction of the P- and N-zones, forming what is called a *depletion layer* (Fig. 9-1). This layer, which

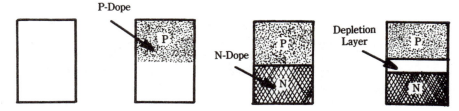

Fig. 9-1. Four stages in the construction of a semiconductor diode, shown in simple diagrammatic form.

contains no free electrons or holes, then acts as a barrier between the P-zone and the N-zone, preventing any further migration of either electrons or holes. In effect, the barrier or depletion layer sets up a potential difference between the two regions and the device remains in a stable state until an external voltage is applied to it.

Figure 9-2 shows what happens when an external voltage is applied to the device. In the first diagram, the + voltage is connected to the P-zone. Provided this voltage is sufficiently high to overcome the potential difference setup in the construction of the device (which may be only a few tenths of a volt (it will repel holes in the P-zone towards the N-zone, and attract electrons in the N-zone into the P-zone. Effectively, the barrier or depletion layer will disappear and current will flow through the device. Voltage applied this way is known as *forward bias.*

If the external voltage is applied the other way, as in the second diagram, the opposite effect is created; i.e., the thickness of the depletion layer increases, thus building up a higher potential in the device, *opposing* the external voltage. The back voltage developed is equal to that of the applied voltage, so no current flows through the device. Voltage applied this way is known as *negative bias.*

The device just described is a semiconductor *diode.* It has the basic characteristic of acting as a conductor when connected to an external voltage one way (forward bias), and as an insulator when connected the other way (reverse bias).

Diode characteristics are described in some detail later on, but the same principles can be applied to explain the working of a *transistor.*

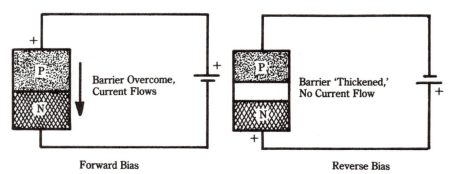

Fig. 9-2. The two modes in which a diode can be operated.

TRANSISTORS

Basically, a transistor is two diodes placed back-to-back with a common middle layer, the middle layer in this case being much thinner than the other two. Two configurations are obviously possible, PNP or NPN (Fig. 9-3). These descriptions are used to describe the two basic types of transistors. Because a transistor contains two seperate semiconductor junctions, it is referred to as a bipolar device, or *bipolar transistor.*

A transistor has three elements, and to operate in a working circuit it is connected with two external voltages or polarities. One external voltage is working effectively as a diode. A transistor will, in fact, work as a diode by using just this connection and forgetting about the top half. An example is the substitution of a transistor for a diode as the detector in a simple radio. It works just as well as a diode because it is working as a diode in this case.

The diode circuit can be given forward or reverse bias. Connected with forward bias, as in the first diagram of Fig. 9-4, drawn for the PNP transistor, current flows from P to the bottom N. If a second voltage is applied to the top and bottom sections of the transistor, with the *same* polarity applied to the bottom, the electrons already flowing through the bottom N section promote a flow of current through the transistor bottom-to-top.

By controlling the degree of doping in the different layers of the transistor during manufacture, this ability to conduct current through the second circuit through the resistor can be very marked. Effectively, when the bottom half is forward biased, the bottom section acts as a generous source of free electrons (and because it emits electrons it is called the *emitter*). These are collected readily by the top half, which is consequently called the *collector,* but the actual amount of current which flows through this particular circuit is controlled by the bias applied at the center layer, which is called the *base.*

Effectively, therefore, there are two separate working circuits when a transistor is working with correctly connected polarities (Fig. 9-5). One is the loop formed by the bias voltage supply encompassing the emitter and base. This is called the *base* circuit or *input* circuit. The second is the circuit formed by the

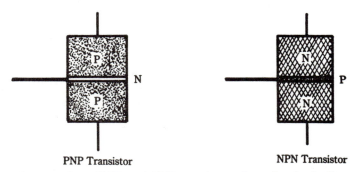

PNP Transistor   NPN Transistor

Fig. 9-3. Construction of PNP and NPN transistors, shown in simple diagrammatic form.

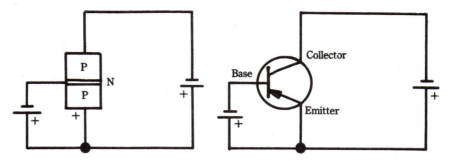

Fig. 9-4. Bias and supply connections to a PNP transistor shown diagrammatically (left) and in symbol form (right).

collector voltage supply and all three elements of the transistor. This is called the *collector* circuit or *output* circuit. (Note: this description applies only when the emitter connection is common to both circuits — known as *common emitter* configuration. This is the most widely used way of connecting transistors, but there are two other alternative configurations — *common base* and *common collector*. The same principles apply in the working of the transistor in each case.)

The particular advantage offered by this circuit is that a relatively small base current can control and instigate a very much larger collector current (or, more correctly, a small input power is capable of producing a much larger output power). In other words, the transistor works as an amplifier.

With this mode of working, the base-emitter circuit is the input side, and the emitter through base to collector circuit is the output side. Although these have a common path through base and emitter, the two circuits are effectively separated by the fact that, as far as polarity of the base circuit is concerned, the base and upper half of the transistor are connected as a reverse biased diode. Hence there is no current flow from the basic circuit into the collector circuit.

For the circuit to work, of course, polarities of both the base and collector circuits have to be correct (forward bias applied to the base circuit, and the collector supply connected so that the polarity of the common element (the

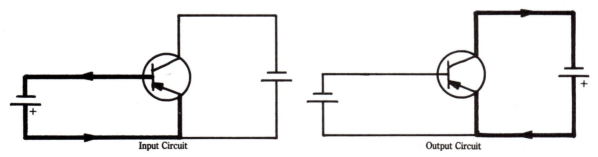

Input Circuit   Output Circuit

Fig. 9-5. The two separate circuits involved in operating a transistor. Direction of current flow is for a PNP transistor.

emitter) is the same from both voltage sources). This also means that the polarity of the voltages must be correct for the type of transistor. In the case of a PNP transistor, as described, the emitter voltage must be positive. It follows that both the base and collector are negatively connected with respect to the emitter. The symbol for PNP transistor has an arrow on the emitter indicating the direction of *current flow;* i.e., always towards the base. (P for positive, with a PNP transistor.)

In the case of an NPN transistor, exactly the same working principles apply but the *polarities* of both supplies are reversed, Fig. 9-6. The emitter is always made negative relative to base and collector. (N for negative in the case of an NPN transistor). This is also inferred by the reverse direction of the arrow on the emitter in the symbol for an NPN transistor; i.e., current flow away from the base.

PRACTICAL DIODES

The typical appearance of a semiconductor diode is shown in Fig. 9-7. The cathode end is usually marked by a red dot or color band, or a + sign, and also usually with a type number consisting of one or more letters followed by figures. This identifies the diode by manufacturer and specific model. Specific type numbers are usually quoted for specific circuit designs, but many circuits are fairly noncritical as regards the type of diode used.

Diodes may also be described in more general terms by the crystal material (germanium or silicon), and by construction. Here, choice can be more important. Germanium diodes start conducting at lower voltages than silicon diodes (about 0.2 to 0.3 volts, as compared with 0.6 volts), but tend to have higher leakage currents when reverse biased, this leakage current increasing fairly substantial with increasing temperature. Thus, the germanium diode is inherently less efficient as a rectifier than a silicon diode, especially if reverse bias current is high enough to produce appreciable heating effect. On the other hand, a germanium diode is preferred to a silicon diode where very low operating voltages are involved because it starts to conduct at a lower forward voltage.

The construction of a diode governs both its current-carrying capabilities

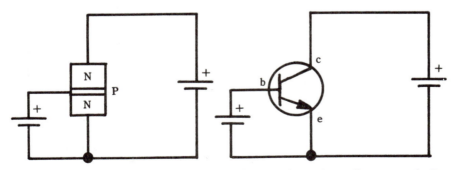

Fig. 9-6. Bias and supply connections to an NPN transistor, shown diagrammatically (left) and in symbolic form (right).

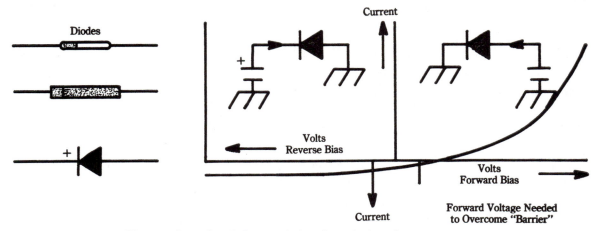

Fig. 9-7. Operational characteristics of a typical semiconductor diode.

when conducting, and its capacitance effect. The larger the *junction area* of a diode, the higher the current it can pass without overheating — for example, this characteristic is desirable in high-power rectifiers. On the other hand, increasing the junction area increases the readiness with which a diode will pass ac due to inherent capacitance effects. To reduce this effect to a minimum, a diode can be made from a single doped crystal (usually N-type), on which the point of a piece of spring wire rests. The end of this wire is given opposite doping (P-type). This reduces the junction area to a minimum, such as a diode being known as a *point-contact* type. It is a favored type for use in circuits carrying high frequency ac signals, and for this reason is sometimes called a *signal diode.*

The typical characteristics of a diode are also shown in simple graphic form in Fig. 9-7. Bias is represented by the voltage applied to the positive side, referred to as *anode voltage.* Current flowing through the diode is referred to as *anode current.*

With forward bias (positive voltage applied to the anode end of the diode), there is at first no anode current until the inherent barrier voltage has been overcome (0.3 volts for a germanium diode, 0.6 volts for a silicon diode — regardless of the construction of either type). Any further increase in anode voltage produces a steep rise of anode current. In practice, it is necessary to limit this current with a resistor or equivalent resistive load in the circuit to prevent the diode being overheated and the junction destroyed.

With reverse bias (negative voltage applied to the anode end of the diode), the only current flowing will be a very small leakage current of the order of microamps only, and normally quite negligible. This leakage current does not increase appreciably with rise in (negative) anode voltage, once it has reached its saturation value.

It will be appreciated that a diode will work in both a dc and an ac circuit. In a dc circuit, it will conduct current if connected with forward bias. If connected the opposite way, it will act as a stop for current flow. An example of this type of use is where a diode is included in a dc circuit — say the output side of a dc power supply — to eliminate any possibility of reverse polarity voltage surges occurring which could damage transistors in the same circuit (see Fig. 26-1).

In an ac circuit a diode will "chop" the applied ac, passing half cycles which are positive with respect to the + end of the diode, and stopping those half cycles which are negative with respect to + end of the diode. This is *rectifier* action, widely used in transforming an ac supply into a dc output. The same action is required of a detector in a radio circuit. Here the current applied to the diode is a mixture of dc and ac. The diode detector transforms this mixed input signal into a varying dc output, the variations following the form of the ac content of the signal.

BASIC TRANSISTOR CIRCUITS

The transistor in common-emitter configuration works as an amplifier, as previously explained. It needs two separate supply voltages — one for bias and the other for the collector — but these do not necessarily have to come from separate batteries. They can be provided by a single supply (battery) taken to the common connection (the emitter) and the collector, and tapping the collector side to apply the necessary forward bias voltage to the base, dropped through a bias resistor.

A basic amplifier circuit then looks like Fig. 9-8. To make the circuit do useful work, the collector current has to be fed through an output load, such as a load resistor. These two diagrams also show clearly input and output as separate entities, and can clarify the point about amplification. The power derived in the output is far greater than that put into the input.

This very simple method of supplying both collector and bias voltages from a single source is known as *current biasing*. It needs only one resistor, and it works. The resistor value is chosen to give a base-emitter voltage of the order of 0.1 to 0.2 volts for germanium transistors; and about 0.6 to 0.7 for silicon transistors. It is not as stable as it should be for many circuits, however, particularly if a germanium transistor is used, so voltage bias is often preferred (Fig. 9-9).

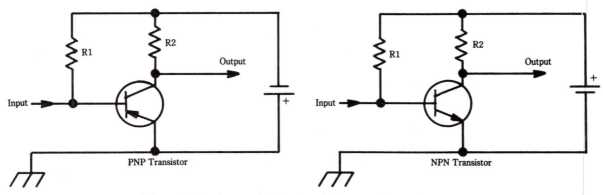

Fig. 9-8. Simple current bias circuits for transistor operation.

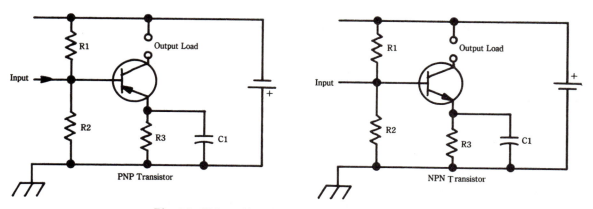

Fig. 9-9. *Voltage bias circuits for transistor operation.*

With voltage bias, two resistors (R1 and R2) are used to work as a divider. A resistor (R3) is also added in the emitter line to provide emitter feedback automatically, to control the bias voltage under varying working conditions. This latter resistor is also usually paralleled with a capacitor to provide further stabilization (but this may be omitted with silicon transistors).

Determination of suitable component values is now more complicated since three resistors are involved. The actual base voltage can be calculated from the following formula:

$$\text{base voltage} = \frac{R2}{(R1 + R2)} \times \text{supply voltage}$$

The emitter voltage is equal to this *less* the voltage between base and emitter (across the transistor). In most cases, a voltage drop of 1 volt in the case of germanium transistors and 3 volts with silicon transistors is the design aim. The emitter resistor (R3) also needs to be quite large so that there are minimal changes in emitter current with any variation in the supply voltage. This can cause a little re-thinking about suitable values for R1 and R2, for the voltage developed across R3 must be very much greater than the voltage developed by the base current across the source resistance formed by the parallel combination of R1 and R2.

TRANSISTOR CONSTRUCTION

The original transistors were made from germanium crystals with point-contact construction. Later types, with considerably improved performance, are of *alloy-junction* or *alloy-diffusion* construction. Silicon transistors are usually made by the *planar* process (silicon planar process). Their characteristics can be further improved by adopting a modified planar process described as *epitaxial*, basically involving a preliminary process of forming an oriented layer (epitaxial layer) of lightly doped silicon over the silicon substrate. The transistor elements are subsequently formed within the layer rather than within the silicon substrate itself (as in the normal planar process). Epitaxial silicon planar transistors have superior characteristics for high frequency applications, notable in rf and i–f circuits for superhet radios.

Germanium and Silicon Transistors

Just like diodes, transistors are made from either germanium or silicon crystals. Germanium transistors have low voltage losses but their characteristics are more liable to vary with temperature, so that the spread of characteristics under which they work in a circuit can be quite wide. They are also limited to a maximum working temperature of about 100°C.

Silicon transistors are generally more stable and can operate at temperatures up to 150°C or more. They have lower leakage losses and higher voltage ratings, and are generally far better suited for use in high frequency circuits.

The Shape of Transistors

Transistors come in all sorts of shapes and sizes. However, the only problem where a specified type of transistor is to be used is correctly identifying the three leads. The position of these can be identified by reference to Fig. 9-10. The most common lead configuration is in line, with a circular case, when the leads follow in logical order—collector, base, emitter, with the collector lead being more widely spaced from the middle (base) lead than the emitter lead, looking at the

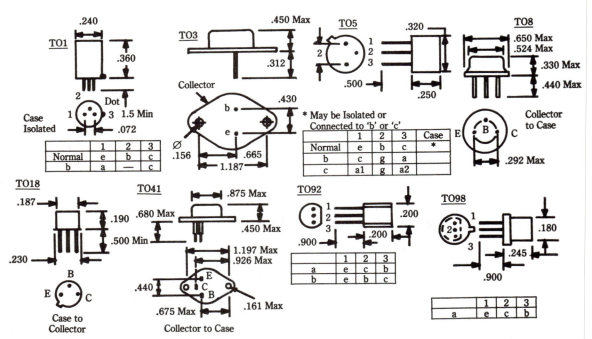

Fig. 9-10. *Some common transistor outlines (diagrams by Electrovalue, all dimensions in inches).*

bottom of the transistor from where the leads emerge. This does not apply when the case is partly circular with one flat side. Here the three leads are equally spaced and with the flat side to the left (and looking at the bottom), the lead arrangement may be bce, cbe, or ebc.

Power transistors are more readily identified by their elongated bottom with two mounting holes. In this case there are only two leads—the emitter and base—and these are normally marked. The collector is connected internally to the can, and so connection to the collector is via one of the mounting bolts or the bottom of the can.

FIELD-EFFECT TRANSISTORS

The *Field-Effect Transistor* (or FET) is really a different type of semiconductor device than a bipolar transistor, with characteristics more like a vacuum tube than a bipolar transistor. Its correct definition is a *unipolar* transistor. The way in which it works can be understood by presenting it in electronic picture form as in Fig. 9-11, where it can be seen that it consists of a *channel* of either P-type or N-type semiconductor material with a collar or *gate* of opposite type material at the center. This forms a semiconductor junction at this point. One end of the channel is called the *source,* and the other end the *drain.*

An FET is connected in a similar manner to a bipolar transistor, with a bias voltage applied between gate and source, and a supply voltage applied across the center of the channel (i.e., between source and drain). The source is thus the common connection between the two circuits. Compared with a bipolar transistor, however, the bias voltage is reversed. That is, the N-gate material of a P-channel FET is biased with positive voltage, and the P-gate material of an N-channel FET is biased with negative voltage (Fig. 9-12). This puts the two system voltages in opposition at the source, which is responsible for the characteristically *high input resistance* of FETs.

The effect of this reverse bias is to form an enlarged depletion layer in the middle of the channel, producing a pinching effect on the flow of electrons through the channel and consequently on the current flow in the source-to-drain

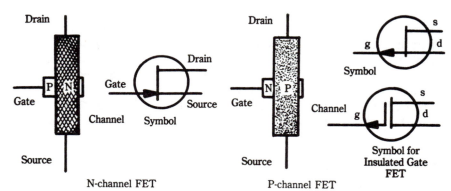

Fig. 9-11. Construction of field-effect transistors shown in simple diagrammatic form, together with appropriate symbols for FETs.

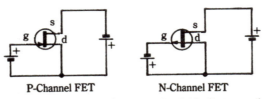

Fig. 9-12. *Basic bias requirements for field-effect transistors.*

circuit. If enough bias voltage is applied, the depletion layer fills the whole gate ("shuts the gate"), causing *pinch off,* when the source-to-drain current falls to zero (in practice nearly to zero, for there is still some leakage). With no bias applied to the gate, the gate is wide open and so maximum current flows.

In effect, then, the amount of reverse bias applied to the gate governs how much of the gate is effectively open for current flow. A relatively small change in gate voltage can produce a large change in source-to-drain current, and so the device works as an amplifier. In this respect, a P-channel FET works very much like a PNP transistor, and an N-channel FET as an NPN transistor. Its main advantage is that it can be made just as compact in size, but can carry much more power. In this respect — and the fact that it has a high input resistance, whereas a bipolar transistor has a low input resistance — it is more like a tube in characteristics than a bipolar transistor. It also has other advantages over a bipolar transistor, notably much lower inherent noise, making it a more favorable choice for an amplifier in a high-quality radio current.

The type of field-effect transistor described is correctly called a junction field-effect transistor, of JFET. There are other types produced by modifying the construction. The insulated-gate field-effect transistor, or IGFET is self-explanatory. The IGFET has even higher input resistance (because the gate is insulated from the channel), and is also more flexible in application since either reverse or forward polarity can be applied to the gate for bias. FETs, of either type, can also be made with two gates. In this case the first gate becomes the *signal gate* (to which the input signal is applied) and the second gate becomes the *control gate,* with similar working to a pentode tube (see Chapter 12).

FETs are also classified by the mode in which they work. A JFET works in the *depletion mode;* i.e., control of the extent of the depletion layer, and thus the "gate opening" being by the application of a bias voltage to the gate. An IGFET can work in this mode, or with opposite bias polarity, in which case the effect is to produce an increasing "gate opening," with enhanced (increased) source-to-drain current. This is called the *enhancement mode.*

An FET designed specifically to work in the enhancement mode has no channel to start with, only a gate. Application of a gate voltage causes a channel to be formed.

The basic circuit of an FET amplifier is very simple, Fig. 9-13 (with polarity drawn for a P-channel FET). Instead of applying a definite negative bias to the gate, a high value resistor (R1) is used to maintain the gate at substantially zero voltage. The value of resistor R2 is then selected to adjust the potential of the source to the required amount *positive* to the gate. The effect is then the same as

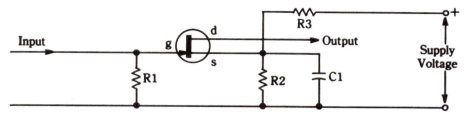

Fig. 9-13. Basic FET amplifier circuit. Performance is generally superior to that of a bipolar transistor amplifier.

if negative bias were applied direct to the gate. This arrangement is also self-compensating with variations in source-to-drain current. The third resistor, R3, is a load resistor for the FET to set the design operating current. Capacitor C1 acts as a conductive path to remove signal currents from the source.

Both junction-type (JFET) and insulated gate (IGFET) field-effect transistors are widely used, the latter having the wider application, particularly in integrated circuits. The metal-oxide semiconductor FET, generally referred to as a MOS-FET, can be designed to work in either mode; i.e., as a depletion MOSFET, or enhancement MOSFET. The former is usually an N-channel device and the latter a P-channel device. P-channel MOSFETS working in the enhancement mode are by far the more popular, mainly because they are easy to produce. In fact, an N-channel MOSFET can be made smaller for the same duty, and has faster switching capabilities, and so really is to be preferred for LSI MOS systems (see also Chapter 13).

10
Neon Lamps, LEDs, and Liquid Crystals

NEON LAMPS

Many circuits use neon lamps, LEDs, or liquid crystal displays. The *neon lamp* is a glow lamp consisting of a glass envelope fitted with two separated electrodes and filled with an inert gas (neon or argon). If connected to a low voltage, the resistance is so high that the neon provides virtually an open circuit, but, if the voltage is increased, there comes a point where the gas ionizes and becomes highly conductive, as well as giving off a glowing light located on the negative electrode. If the gas is neon, the glow is orange in color. Argon is sometimes used as the gas, in which case the glow is blue.

The characteristic performance of a neon lamp is shown in Fig. 10-1. The voltage at which the neon starts to glow is called the initial breakdown voltage. Once this has been reached and the bulb triggered into firing (glowing), the voltage drop across the lamp will remain virtually constant regardless of any increase in current in the circuit. At the same time, the area of glow increases with increasing current, up to the point where the entire surface of the negative electrode is covered by glow. Any further increase in current then pushes the neon into an arc condition, where the glow changes to a blue-white point of light on the negative electrode and results in the rapid destruction of the lamp.

To operate a neon lamp successfully, therefore, it is necessary to have enough voltage for the neon to fire, and, after that, enough resistance in the circuit to limit the current to that which will ensure that the lamp remains operating in the normal glow region. Because the resistance of the neon itself is very low after

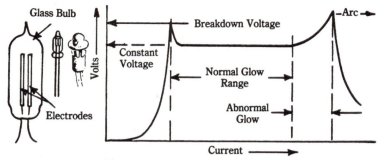

Fig. 10-1. Typical neon lamp construction and characteristic performance.

firing, this requires the use of a resistor in series with the lamp, known as a *ballast resistor*. Typically the firing, or breakdown, voltage may be anything from about 60 to 100 volts (in some cases even higher). The continuous current rating is quite low, usually between 0.1 and 10 milliamps. The series resistor value is chosen accordingly, related to the voltage of the supply to which the neon will be connected. In the case of neon lamps to be operated off a 250 volt (mains) supply, a 220 kΩ resistor is normally adequate (see Fig. 10-2). With some commercial lamps, the resistor may actually be built into the body of the assembly.

Lacking any specific information on this subject, it can be assumed that a neon lamp has no resistance when glowing, but drops 80 volts. A suitable value for a ballast resistor can be calculated on this basis related to the actual voltage of the supply to be used, and assuming a safe current of 0.2 milliamps, for example.

For a 250-volt supply, the resistor has to drop 250 − 80 = 170 volts. The current through resistor and neon (in series) is to be 0.2 mA. Therefore:

$$\text{Resistance} = \frac{\text{volts}}{\text{amps}}$$

$$= \frac{170}{0.2 \times 1/1000}$$

$$= 850 \text{ k}\Omega, \text{ or about } 1 \text{ M}\Omega$$

This should be playing safe with most commercial lamps. If the glow is not very bright, the value of the ballast resistor can be decreased to operate lamp farther

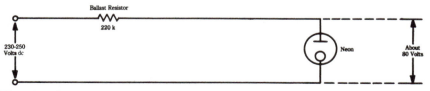

Fig. 10-2. In a practical circuit, a neon lamp is always connected in series with a ballast resistor to limit current flow.

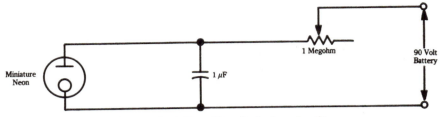

Fig. 10-3. Adjustable rate flasher circuit.

along the normal glow region. However, the resistance should never be decreased so much that the whole of the negative electrode is covered by glow; this indicates that the lamp is becoming overloaded and approaching the arc condition.

Another point about the strength of the glow light is that it normally appears *brighter* in light than in dark. In fact, in complete darkness the glow may be erratic and/or require a higher breakdown voltage to start it. Some lamps have a minute trace of radioactive gas added to the inert gas to stimulate ionization making this particular effect unnoticeable.

Because of the constant-voltage characteristics of a neon lamp under normal glow conditions, it can be used as a voltage stabilizing device. Thus, in the circuit shown in Fig. 10-2, the output tapped from each side of the lamp is a source of constant voltage as long as the lamp remains working in the normal glow region. This voltage is the same as the nominal breakdown voltage of the lamp.

The use of a neon lamp as a *flasher* in a relaxation oscillator circuit has already been described (Fig. 6-3, Chapter 6). A variation on this is shown in Fig. 10-3, using a 1 megohm potentiometer as the ballast resistor and two 45-volt or four 22½-volt dry batteries as the source of supply. The potentiometer is adjusted until the lamp lights. The control is then turned the other way until the lamp just goes out. Leaving the potentiometer in this position, the lamp should then flash at regular intervals determined by the value of the capacitor.

An adaption of this circuit is shown in Fig. 10-4, where the circuit is switched by a Morse key. Phones can be connected across the point shown to listen into the Morse signals, which are also visible as a flashing light. An ordinary bulb would work just as well as a visible indicator (and with a much lower voltage required), but in this case the signals would only be heard as clicks. With the neon

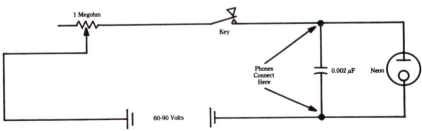

Fig. 10-4. Morse code flasher circuit.

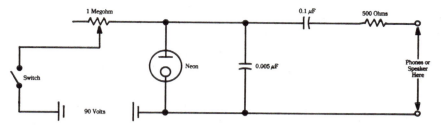

Fig. 10-5. Simple tone generator based on an NE-2 miniature neon lamp.

circuit, the actual oscillation of the relaxation oscillator is heard. The time constant of the circuit is governed by the value of the capacitor and the setting of the ballast potentiometer.

A further extension of the use of a neon lamp as an *oscillator* in a relaxation oscillator circuit is shown in Fig. 10-5. This is a true signal generator circuit, the output of which should be audible in headphones or even a small loudspeaker, with the tone adjustable by the potentiometer.

Neon flashers can be made to work in random fashion (again see Chapter 6), or sequentially. A circuit for a sequential flasher is shown in Fig. 10-6. More stages can be added to this circuit, if desired, taking the connection of C3 to the last stage.

Finally, an *astable multivibrator* circuit is shown in Fig. 10-7, using two lamps. These will flash on and off in sequence at a rate determined by R1 and R2 (which should be equal in value) and C1.

As a general guide to flasher timing, increasing the value of the ballast resistor or the capacitor in the relaxation oscillator circuit slows the rate of flashing; and vice versa. To preserve the life of a typical lamp, however, the value of ballast resistor used should not be less than about 100 kΩ; and best results in simple relaxation oscillator circuits can usually be achieved by keeping the capacitor value below 1 microfarad.

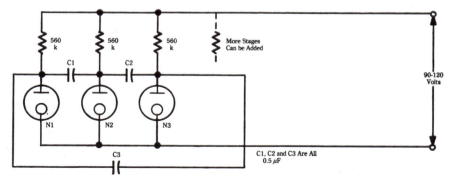

Fig. 10-6. Sequential flasher using NE-2 miniature neon lamps (or equivalent).

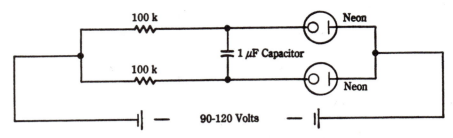

Fig. 10-7. Astable multivibrator circuit, each neon flashing in turn.

LEDs

LED is short for Light-Emitting Diode. This is essentially a two element semiconductor device where the energy produced by conduction in a specific direction is radiated as light. The intensity of the light is governed by the current flowing through the diode. In these respects, LEDs are somewhat similar to neon lamps, but they light at very much lower forward voltages (typically 1.6 to 2 volts) and can generally draw higher forward currents without burning out (typically 20 mA). Originally the color of light emitted by LEDs was red, but now orange, yellow and green LEDs are also available.

Again like neon lamps, an LED is invariably associated with a ballast resistor in series to limit the voltage applied to the LED and the current flowing through it. The value of resistor required is:

$$R = \frac{V_s - V_f}{I_f}$$

where:

V_s = dc supply voltage
V_f = rated forward voltage of the LED
I_f = rated forward current of the LED at specified forward voltage

Thus, for operating off, say, a 6-volt supply, a typical value for the ballast resistor would be $(6 - 2)/(20 \times 10^{-3}) = 200$ ohms.

In the case of an ac supply, a diode is connected in inverse parallel with the LED and the resistor value required is one half that given by the above formula, see also Fig. 10-8.

LEDs are often used in groups, such as in calculators, or digital instruments. The most common form is a seven-segment display and associated point, see Fig. 10-9. Such a display can light up numerals from 0 to 9, depending on the individual segments energized, with or without the decimal point lighted. Each segment (or point) is, of course, an individual LED.

Specific advantages of LEDs are that they require only low voltages, are fast switching and can be produced in very small sizes, if required. The most widely used seven-segment displays, for example, give figures which are 0.3 in. or

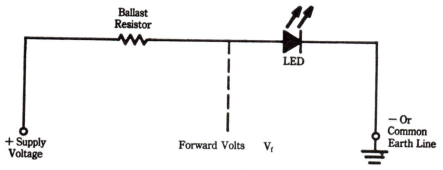

Fig. 10-8. LEDs are connected with a ballast resistor in series to drop the supply voltage in the required forward voltage. Note the symbol for an LED (light-emitting diode).

0.5 in. high. Power consumption is relatively low, but an 8-digit seven-segment display could have a maximum power consumption in excess of 2 watts (e.g., $8 \times 7 \times 20$ mA at 2 volts).

This can place restrictions on their applications to displays powered by miniature batteries, as in digital watches. To provide a reasonable battery life, the display is normally left in open circuit and only switched on for the short period when it is required to read the display.

LIQUID CRYSTAL

The *liquid crystal* overcomes this particular power limitation since it can be activated by very much lower power (actually a tiny amount of *heat,* which can be produced by an equally tiny amount of electrical energy). Also, the display can be made much larger while still working at microscopic power levels, so that it can be left on all the time. The liquid crystal has its disadvantages, however. It is far less bright than an LED display, and also suffers from dark effect (like a neon lamp in this respect). Thus to be legible in dim light, the liquid crystal display needs to be illuminated by a separate light course.

Liquid crystal displays operate with low voltage and low current. Current drain can be as little as 1 microamp (1 μA) per segment. A later development, the field-effect liquid crystal, can work on even lower voltages drawing microscopic currents (of the order of 300 nA), again making them an attractive choice for battery-powered displays. The field-effect liquid crystal also has better contrast, giving a black image on a light background.

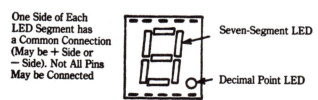

Fig. 10-9. Typical LED display, as used in calculators. The eight LEDs are internally connected to a common cathode or common anode pin.

11
Other Components

Other types of components likely to be met in electronic circuits are described in this chapter for easy reference. Many are variations on standard components previously described, but with different working characteristics. The diode family, for example, is particularly numerous.

THE DIODE FAMILY

Diodes are used in a wide variety of applications. See Chapter 9 for information on general purpose diodes.

Zener Diodes

The Zener diode is a silicon junction diode. When reverse bias voltage is applied and increased, there comes a point where the diode suddenly acts as a conductor rather than an insulator. The point at which this occurs is called the *breakdown voltage* (or Zener point). Once reached, it remains constant, even if the reverse bias voltage is increased. In other words, once reverse biased to, or beyond, the breakdown voltage, the voltage drop across the diode remains constant at its breakdown voltage value, regardless of the actual current flowing through the diode.

This important characteristic makes Zener diodes particularly useful as a source of constant dc voltage, or for stabilizing a supply voltage, using the type of connection shown in Fig. 11-1. A series resistor (R) is necessary to limit the

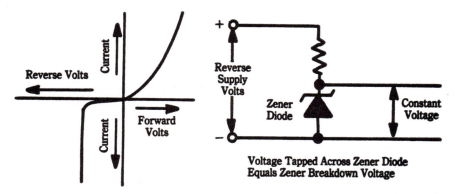

Fig. 11-1. A Zener diode, working with reverse bias, breaks down at a specific reverse voltage. Connected as shown, it can be used as a source of constant voltage supply. Note the symbol for a Zener diode.

amount of current flowing through the diode; otherwise, it could be burned out. Regardless of the value of the input volts, the voltage dropped across the Zener diode remains constant, so any variations in the input voltage do not affect the output voltage tapped from across the Zener diode. This voltage is the breakdown voltage of the diode, which may range from about 2.7 volts up to 100 volts or more, depending on the construction of the Zener diode. If the input voltage falls below the breakdown voltage, of course, the Zener diode will stop conducting and break the circuit.

Performance of a Zener diode as a voltage-stabilizing device is limited only by the power rating, which may be quite low — under 500 mW for the small Zener diodes, but up to 5 watts or more in larger sizes. Its stability is also affected by the heating effect of the actual current flowing through it, causing a shift in the breakdown voltage, so the nominally constant voltage can vary with working temperature. If this is likely to be troublesome (the type of Zener diode used has a fairly high temperature coefficient of resistance), then connecting two similar diodes in series can greatly improve the temperature coefficient. Also, the power rating is increased.

Varicap Diodes

Another special type of diode is the *varicap* or *varactor*. These behave as capacitors with a high Q (see Chapter 6) when biased in the reverse direction, the actual capacitance value being dependent on the bias voltage applied. Typical applications are the automatic control of tuned circuits, "electronic tuning," adjusting capacity in the circuit, and thus resonant frequency, in response to changes in signal voltage; automatic frequency control of local oscillator circuits in superhets and TV circuits; and also as frequency doublers and multipliers. Symbols for a varicap are shown in Fig. 11-2.

Fig. 11-2. Alternative symbols for a varicap.

Tunnel Diodes

The *tunnel diode* is another type with special characteristics, unlike that of any other semiconductor device. It is constructed like an ordinary diode but the crystal is more heavily doped, resulting in an extremely thin barrier (potential layer). As a consequence, electrons can *tunnel* through this barrier.

This makes the tunnel diode a good conductor with both forward and reverse voltage. Behavior, however, is quite extraordinary when the forward voltage is increased, see Fig. 11-3. Forward current at first rises with increasing forward voltage until it reaches a peak value. With increasing forward voltage, current then drops, to reach a minimum, or *valley*, value. After that it rises again with further increase in forward voltage. Worked in the region from peak voltage to valley voltage, the tunnel diode exhibits *negative resistance* characteristics. Another interesting feature is that any forward current value between peak and valley value is obtainable three times (at three different forward voltages).

Tunnel diodes have a particular application for very high speed switching, with a particular application to pulse and digital circuitry, e.g., digital computers.

Schottky Diode

The *Schottky diode* is a metal semiconductor diode, formed by integrated circuit techniques and generally incorporated in ICs as a clamp between base and emitter of a transistor to prevent saturation. Voltage drop across such a diode is

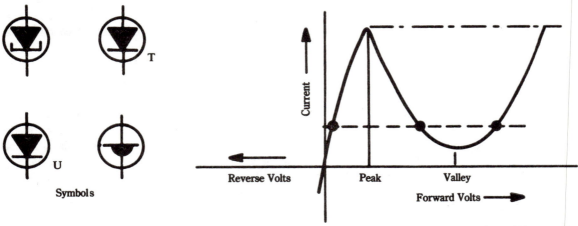

Fig. 11-3. Symbols (left) and characteristic performance of a tunnel diode. From peak to valley it exhibits negative resistance.

Fig. 11-4. Typical circuit for a Schottky diode (left) and the equivalent single component, a Schottky transistor.

less than that of a conventional semiconductor diode for the same forward current. Otherwise, its characteristics are similar to that of a germanium diode. A typical circuit employing a Schottky diode is shown in Fig. 11-4.

For circuits using a Schottky diode as a clamping device associated with a transistor, diode and transistor may be produced at the same time in processing the transistor. This combination device is called a *Schottky transistor* (see *also* Fig. 11-4).

Photodiodes

It is a general characteristic of semiconductor diodes that if they are reverse biased and the junction is illuminated, the reverse current flow varies in proportion to the amount of light. This effect is utilized in the *photodiode* which has a clear window through which light can fall on one side of the crystal and across the junction of the P- and N-zones.

In effect, such a diode works in a circuit as a variable resistance, the amount of resistance offered by the diode being dependent on the amount of light falling on the diode. In the dark, the photodiode will have normal reverse working characteristics; i.e., provide almost infinitely high resistance with no current flow. At increasing levels of illumination, resistance becomes proportionately reduced, thus allowing increasing current to flow through the diode. The actual amount of current is proportionate to the illumination only, provided there is sufficient reverse voltage. In other words, once past the "knee" of the curve (Fig. 11-5), the diode current at any level of illumination does not increase substantially with increasing reverse voltage.

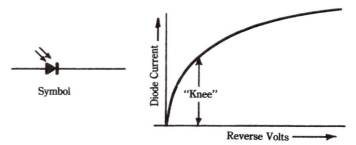

Fig. 11-5. Symbol (left); and characteristic performance of a photodiode.

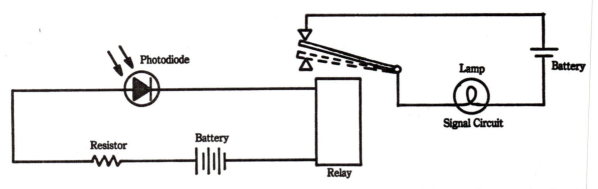

Fig. 11-6. *Photodiode used as a light switch. The rise in current when the diode is illuminated makes the relay pull in completing an external circuit through the relay contacts.*

Photodiodes are extremely useful for working as light-operated switches as shown in Fig. 11-6. They have a fairly high switching speed, so they can also be used as counters, counting each interruption of a beam of light as a pulse of current.

There are two other types of light-sensitive diodes: the photovoltaic diode and the light-emitting diode (LED). The *photovoltaic diode* generates voltage when illuminated by light, the resulting current produced in an associated circuit being proportional to the intensity of the light. This property is utilized in the construction of light meters. The amount of current produced by a photodiode can be very small, and so some amplification of the current may be introduced in such a circuit. Special types of photodiodes are known as *photocells* and are generally more suitable for use as practical light meters.

The *light-emitting diode* works in an opposite manner of a photodiode. It emits light when a current is passed through it. Light-emitting diodes are described in Chapter 10.

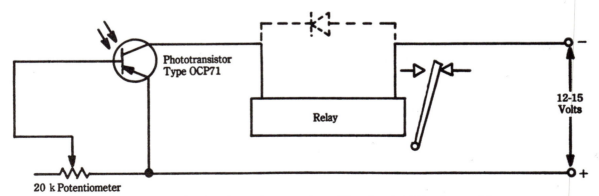

Fig. 11-7. *Practical light switch circuit using a phototransistor. The relay should be of a sensitive type and adjusted to pull in at about 2 milliamps. The potentiometer is a sensitivity control.*

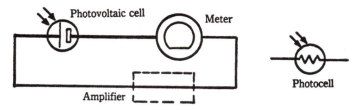

Fig. 11-8. Basic photovoltaic diode circuit. Shown on the right is the symbol for a photocell.

THE PHOTOTRANSISTOR

The phototransistor is much more sensitive than the photodiode to changes in level of illumination, thus making a better switching device where fairly small changes in level of illumination are present and must be detected. It works both as a photoconductive device and an *amplifier* of the current generated by incident light. A simple circuit employing a phototransistor is shown in Fig. 11-7.

A phototransistor and a light-emitting diode (see Chapter 10) may be combined in a single envelope as an *optoisolator*. In this case, the LED provides the source of illumination to which the phototransistor reacts. It can be used in two working modes—either as a *photodiode* (Fig. 11-9) with the emitter of the transistor part left disconnected, or as a *phototransistor* (Fig. 11-9). In both cases, working is governed by the current flowing through the LED section.

Solar Cells

The photodiode is a *photovoltaic* cell. Light falling on its junction produces a voltage. This voltage measured an open circuit (e.g., with a very-high-resistance voltmeter connected across the cell), is known as the *photovoltaic potential* of the cell. In this respect it is like a dry battery. Connected to an external load, the cell voltage will fall to some lower value dependent on the resistance in the circuit (see Chapter 18).

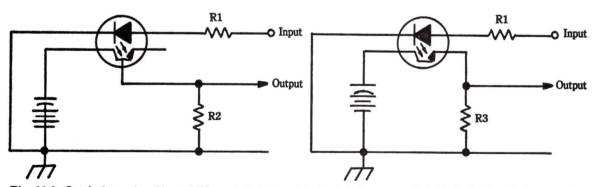

Fig. 11-9. Optoisolator (combined LED and phototransistor), operating as a photodiode (left) and phototransistor (right).

Photovoltaic cells develop a potential when illuminated by any source of light. The photovoltaic potential depends on the construction of the cell, but for any given cell, is proportional to the intensity of the light.

The solar cell is a photovoltaic cell (silicon photodiode) designed to respond to sunlight. Modern photovoltaic cells (commonly called *solar cells*) are commercially available in cell sizes up to 4 inches in diameter with an output of .45 volts at 1.5 amps each in bright sunlight.

To get higher voltages and currents from a solar battery, a number of cells have to be used connected in series-parallel. Series connection gives a cell voltage equal to the sum of the individual cell voltages. Parallel connection gives a current equal to the sum of the individual cell currents.

Suppose, for example, the solar battery was intended to operate a circuit requiring a nominal 2 volts and give a current of 15 milliamps through a 100 ohm load. From the voltage consideration, number of cells required = 2 divided by 500 mV (voltage per cell) = 4 cells.

From current considerations, number of cells required = 15 divided by 3 (current per cell) = 15 cells.

The solar battery required would thus have to consist of five rows each of four cells, each row consisting of four cells connected in series, and each row being connected together in parallel (Fig. 11-10).

A single solar cell can be used to measure solar power (the strength of sunlight at any time). The cell is simply mounted on a suitable panel, sensitive side (negative side) facing outwards, and the two cell leads connected to a 0-500 milliammeter, Fig. 11-11A. Directed towards the sun, the meter then gives a reading representative of the strength of the sunlight. To measure maximum or peak radiation, point the cell directly towards the sun. To use the instrument as a device for plotting solar energy (as a *radiometer*) the panel should be pointed due south and tilted upwards at an angle approximately 10 degrees more than the local latitude. Readings are then taken at intervals throughout the day, indicating how much solar energy the panel is receiving.

If the meter readings are very low, add a shunt resistor across the meter

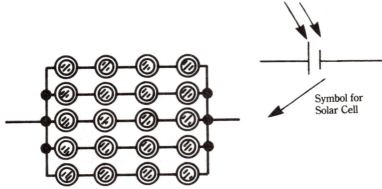

Symbol for
Solar Cell

Fig. 11-10. Connections for a 2-volt solar battery to give a current of 15 milliamps through a 100 ohm load.

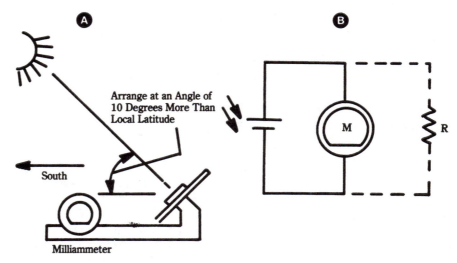

Fig. 11-11. Aligning a photocell to measure solar energy (left). The circuit on the right is a complete solar energy meter, a 0-500 milliamp type.

(shown in broken lines) in Fig. 11-11B. This needs to be a very low value (1 or 2 ohms only). Find a suitable value by trial and error to give near maximum meter reading in the brightest summer sunlight.

RECTIFIERS

The conventional diode is a rectifier, its maximum forward current capabilities being determined mainly by its junction area. For signal rectification, point contact diodes are usually preferred (see Chapter 9), which may limit maximum forward current to 30 to 50 mA, depending on type. Where higher powers are required, larger rectifier diodes can be used, with maximum current ratings up to several hundred amps.

In the case of power supplies (Chapter 26), four diodes in bridge configuration are normally used for full-wave rectification. Physically, this does not mean that four separate diodes have to be connected up (Fig. 8-5). Bridge rectifiers are available as integral units. The average voltage output from such a bridge is 0.9 times the root-mean-square voltage developed across the secondary of the transformer, less the voltage drop across the rectifier itself.

For high voltage applications, semiconductor diodes (usually silicon) can be placed in a series arrangement to increase the overall PIV (peak inverse voltage) rating. For example, if you need a diode with a PIV of 500 volts, you can connect 5 diodes in series, each having an individual PIV of only 100 volts. The maximum current rating in such an arrangement is the lowest maximum current rating of any individual diode in the string. Selenium rectifiers, originally widely used for voltages up to about 100 rms, have now been virtually replaced by silicon diodes.

Silicon controlled rectifiers or SCRs (also known as thyristors) are silicon diodes with an additional electrode called a *gate*. If a bias voltage is applied to the gate to keep it at or near the same potential as the cathode of the diode, the thyristor behaves as if working with reverse voltage with both directions of applied voltage, so only a small leakage current flows. If the gate is biased to be more positive than the cathode, the thyristor behaves as a normal diode. In other words, the gate can be used to turn the rectifier on (by positive bias on the gate), thus enabling forward current to be controlled (e.g., preventing forward current flowing over any required portion of a half cycle).

A triac is a further variation on this principle, providing bidirectional control. It is virtually a double-ended thyristor which can be triggered with either positive or negative gate pulses.

Structurally, an SCR is a four-layer diode, with connections to the inner layers. The terminal connected to the P-region nearest the cathode is the cathode gate, and the terminal connected to the N-region nearest the anode the anode gate, (Fig. 11-12). Both gates are brought out in a triac. Only the cathode gate is brought out in a thyristor. Both devices are essentially ac switches. The thyristor is effective only on one half of an ac voltage, and the triac is effective on both halves.

THERMISTORS

A thermistor is designed specifically to exploit the characteristic of many semiconductor materials to show marked reduction in resistance with increasing temperature. This is the opposite effect exhibited by most metal conductors where resistance increases with increasing temperature.

The obvious value of a thermistor is to balance the effect of changes in temperature on component characteristics in a particular circuit, i.e., work as a compensating device by automatic adjustment of its resistance, down (or up), as working temperatures rise or fall and resistances of other components rise or fall. Compensation for temperature changes of as much as 100°C are possible with thermistors—a typical application being shown in Fig. 11-13. Here, the

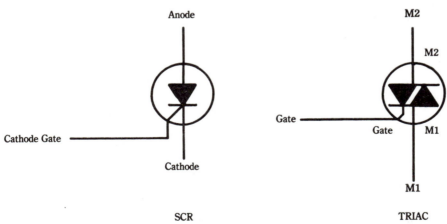

Fig. 11-12. Symbols for SCR and triac.

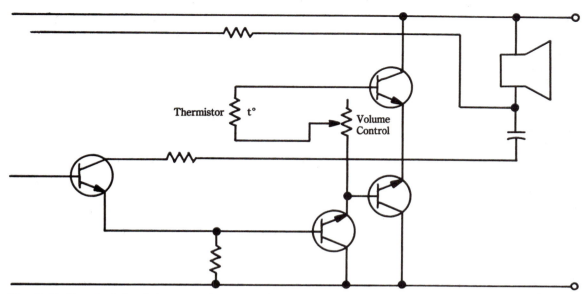

Fig. 11-13. *Practical circuit incorporating a thermistor to counteract fluctuations in value of other resistors in the circuit due to heating effects or temperature changes.*

thermistor is used to stabilize the working values of the resistors in an audio amplifier circuit.

Another use for a thermistor is to eliminate current surges when a circuit is switched on. Certain circuits offer relatively low resistance when first switched on, which could produce a damaging surge of high current. A thermistor in the supply line with a relatively high cold resistance limits the initial peak current surge. Its resistance value then drops appreciably as it warms up so that the voltage dropped across the thermistor under normal working conditions is negligible.

Thermistors are made in the form of rods, looking rather like a carbon rod, sintered from mixtures of metallic oxides. They are not made from the usual semiconductor materials (germanium and silicon) since the characteristics of a thermistor made from these materials would be too sensitive to impurities.

12
Tubes

Tubes (vacuum-tubes) are distinctly old-fashioned in these days of transistors and other semiconductor devices, yet they are still widely used in commercial circuits, especially where high power levels are involved.

The basic form of a tube is an evacuated glass envelope containing two electrodes — a cathode and anode. The cathode is heated, causing electrons to be emitted which are attracted by the anode, thus causing current to flow through the tube in the basic circuit shown in Fig. 12-1 (first diagram).

The original form of heating was by a separate low-voltage supply to a wire *filament* forming the cathode. The later form is a cathode in the form of a tube with a separate heater element passing through it. This is known as an *indirectly* heated cathode, particular advantages being that there is no voltage drop across the cathode (and thus electron emission is more uniform), and also the heating filament can be connected to a separate ac supply, if necessary, rather than requiring a separate dc supply. Otherwise, the working of the tube is identical. Both require a filament supply and a separate high voltage supply.

DIODES

The simplest form of tube shown in Fig. 12-1 is called a diode, because it has two internal elements. Its working characteristics are that when the cathode is heated, application of voltage across the anode and cathode will cause a current to flow, the current value increasing with anode voltage up to the *saturation point* (Fig. 12-2).

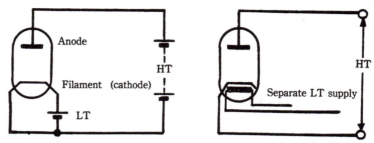

Fig. 12-1. Diode vacuum tubes with directly heated filament (left) and indirectly heated filament (right).

A diode tube only conducts current in one direction. In other words, it is a rectifier just like its solid-state counterpart (see Chapter 9).

Note that in this working circuit a load resistor is included in the circuit. Without any external load in circuit, all the power input to a tube would be used up in heating the anode. To do useful work, a tube must work with a load of some kind or another, so that power is developed in the load. To work efficiently, most of the input power must do useful work in the load, rather than in heating the anode. Thus the voltage drop across the load should be much higher than the voltage drop across the tube.

TRIODES AND TETRODES

If a third element, known as a *grid,* is inserted between the cathode and anode, a negative *bias voltage* can be applied to this to control the working of the tube and thus the anode current. Such a tube is known as a *triode.* A basic circuit is shown in Fig. 12-3, with characteristic performance curves. The advantage of this mode of working is that a small change in *bias* voltage (or voltage applied to the grid) is just as effective as a large change in *anode* voltage in bringing about a change in anode current.

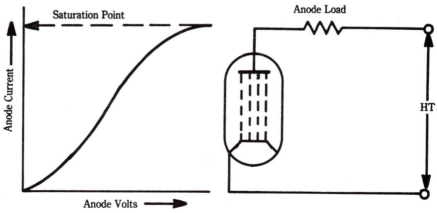

Fig. 12-2. Typical diode characteristics (left). To do useful work, the anode current must flow through a load resistor.

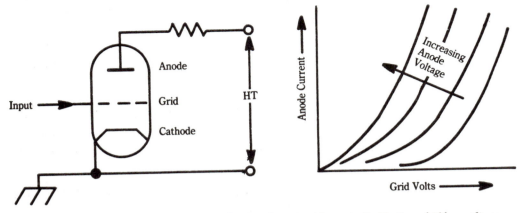

Fig. 12-3. A triode is a three-element tube. Anode current is controlled by the grid bias voltage.

The triode is a particularly versatile type of tube which can readily be made to work as an *amplifier* or an *oscillator* (an oscillator is really only an amplifier working with excessive feedback producing self-sustained oscillation). It does, however, have certain limitations which may be disadvantageous in certain circuits. One is that the inherent capacitance generated between the anode and grid can materially affect the performance of an amplifier circuit where the presence of this capacitance is aggravated by what is called "Miller effect." To overcome this particular limitation, a positively biased second grid called a *screen grid* can be inserted between the grid and anode. This acts as an electrostatic shield to prevent capacitive coupling between the grid and anode. Such a four-element tube is known as a *tetrode* (Fig. 12-4A).

Even the tetrode is not without its faults. The cure for one limitation (inter-electrode capacitance) has produced another fault. The screen grid tends to attract *secondary emission* electrons bouncing off the anode because it has a positive bias, whereas in the triode the only grid present is negatively biased and tends to repel secondary-emission electrons straight back to the anode.

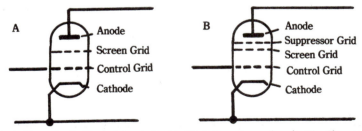

Fig. 12-4. Tetrode (left) and pentode (right) tubes shown in simple diagrammatic form.

PENTODES

To overcome this effect in a tetrode, a fifth element called a *suppressor grid* is added, inserted between the screen grid and the anode (Fig. 12-4B). This acts as a shield to prevent secondary emission electrons being attracted by the screen grid. A five-element valve of this type is called a *pentode*.

THE CATHODE-RAY TUBE

The cathode-ray tube has the same number of elements as a triode (heated cathode, anode, and grid) but works in an entirely different manner. Instead of electrons emitted by the cathode flowing to the anode, they are ejected in the form of a narrow stream to impinge on the far end of the tube, which is coated with a luminescent material or phosphor, so producing a point of light. This point of light can be stationary or moving. Its direction after emission from the far end of the tube is influenced by the magnetic field created by two additional sets of electrodes or plates positioned at right angles (Fig. 12-5). This plates are designated X and Y. Voltage applied to the X plate displaces the light spot in a horizontal direction; voltage applied to the Y plates displaces the light spot in a vertical direction. (See Chapter 23 for a more detailed description of the working of a cathode-ray tube.)

A cathode-ray tube can be used as a voltmeter, with the advantage that it puts no load on the circuit being measured. Cathode and anode are connected to a separate supply, the voltage to be measured being connected to the Y plates. A dc voltage displaces the spot a proportional distance above (or below) the center line of the tube. If the voltage applied is ac, the light spot travels up and down at the frequency of the supply, which is usually too fast for the spot to be identified as such, so it shows a trace of light in the form of a vertical line, Fig. 12-6. The length of this line is proportional to the peak-to-peak voltage of the ac.

The more usual application of the cathode-ray tube is in an oscilloscope, where a voltage which is increasing at a steady rate is applied to the X plates. If another varying voltage is then applied to the Y plates, the spot draws a *time graph* of this voltage, or a picture of the *waveform* of that voltage. The X plate varying voltage supply is usually arranged so that once the spot has swept the width of the screen it returns to the start and repeats the picture over and over again.

The rate of repetition is determined by the time base of the X plate circuit, this being one of the most important features in oscilloscope design in order to

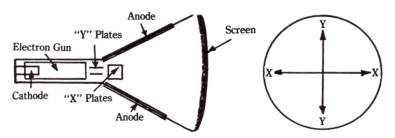

Fig. 12-5. Simplified diagram of a cathode-ray tube.

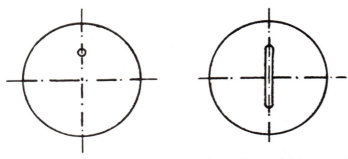

Fig. 12-6. Simple display of dc voltage (left) and ac voltage (right) on a cathode-ray tube. The vertical displacement is a measure of the value of the voltage concerned.

achieve a steady trace at the required frequency. Separate shift controls are also usually provided for both X and Y deflection so that the starting point of the light spot can be set at any point on the screen. Amplifier circuits are also essential in order to be able to adjust the strength input signals applied to the Y plates, and also the X plates if these are also to be fed with an input signal instead of the time base. With these refinements (and others) the cathode-ray oscilloscope is one of the most useful tools an electronics engineer can have.

13
Integrated Circuits

An integrated circuit, or IC, consists of a single-crystal chip of silicon on which has been formed resistors, capacitors, diodes, and transistors (as required) to make a complete circuit with all necessary interconnections; the whole lot in micro-miniature form (Fig. 13-1). The cost of an IC chip is surprisingly low, considering how complicated it can be. This is due to the large quantities processed at a time. A 1-inch square wafer, for example, may be divided into 50 individual IC chips. A single LSI (large scale integration) chip can contain thousands of components in an area smaller than the top of a pencil eraser.

Apart from the convenience of having a complete circuit in such a small size, ICs are very reliable because all components are fabricated simultaneously and there are no soldered joints.

Diodes and transistors in an IC chip are formed by exactly the same process used for producing individual diodes and transistors, but in very much reduced physical size. Integrated resistors are much simpler. They can be a very tiny area of sheet material produced by diffusion in the crystal, or thin film (a millionth of an inch thick) deposited on the silicon layer. Practical resistor ranges which can be achieved are 10 ohms to 50 kilohms, depending on the actual construction, in an area too tiny to see with the naked eye.

Capacitors are a little more difficult. They can either be based on a diode-type formulation (diffused junction capacitor) or on thin-film construction (MOS capacitor). Typical capacitor values achieved are 0.2 pF per thousandth of an inch area. Usual maximum values are 400 pF for diffused junction capacitors, and 800 pF for MOS capacitors.

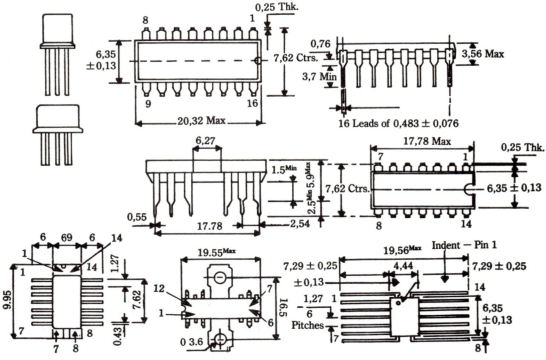

Fig. 13-1. Some examples of the physical appearance of ICs.

Inductances are another story. They cannot — as yet — be produced satisfactorily on silicon substrates using semi-conductor or thin-film techniques. Hence, if a circuit specifically needs an inductance in it, the corresponding IC chip is produced without it and an individual inductance is connected externally to the IC.

This is common practice in the application of many ICs. The IC is not absolutely complete. It contains the bulk of the components, but the final circuit is completed by connecting up additional components externally. It is also usually designed as a multi-purpose circuit with a number of alternative connection points giving access to different parts of the circuit, so that when used with external components, connection can be made to appropriate points to produce a whole variety of different working circuits.

MONOLITHIC AND HYBRID ICS

Integrated circuits built into a single crystal are known as *monolithic* ICs, and incorporate all necessary interconnections. The problem of electrical isolation of individual components is solved by the processing technique used.

In another type of construction, individual components, or complete circuits, are attached to the same substrate but physically separated. Interconnections are then made by bonded wires. This type of construction is known as a *hybrid circuit.*

MSI AND LSI

MSI stands for medium-scale integration; and LSI for large-scale integration, referring to the *component density* achieved. For example, a density of 50 components per chip is typical for many commercially available integrated circuits. These fall into the category of MSI chips, defined as having a component density of more than 12 but not more than 100 components per chip. LSI chips have a much higher component density — as many as 1,000,000 components per chip.

This is largely due to the considerable saving in component sizes possible using thin-film techniques instead of diffusion techniques, particularly in the case of transistors. For example, an MOS transistor can be one tenth the size of a diffused bipolar transistor for the same duty. Hence many more components can be packed into the same size of IC chip.

OP AMPS

The operational amplifier or *op amp* is a type of IC used as the basic building block for numerous analog circuits and systems — amplifiers, computers, filters, voltage-to-current or current-to-voltage converters, modulators, comparators, waveform generators, etc. It is a typical, almost complete circuit, used in conjunction with a few external components to complete the actual circuit required. Three typical circuits using a simple op amp chip are shown in Fig. 13-2.

DIGITAL SYSTEMS ICS

Digital systems work in discrete steps, or virtually by counting in terms of binary numbers. Basically, this calls for the use of logic elements or *gates,* together with a memory unit capable of storing binary numbers, generally called a *flip-flop.* Thus, a digital system is constructed from gates and flip-flops. Integrated circuits capable of performing the functions of binary addition, counting, decoding, multiplexing (date selection), memory and register, digital-to-analog conversion, and analog-to-digital conversion, are the basic building blocks for digital systems.

These give rise to a considerable number of different logic families, which are difficult to understand without a knowledge of logic itself. Most of them are NAND gates because all logic functions (except memory) can be performed by this type of gate, the function of NAND being explained very simply with reference to Fig. 13-3. A and B are two separate inputs to the *gate,* and Y is the output. There will be an output if there is input at either A or B, but *not* when there is input simultaneously at A and B — NOT A AND B (NOT-AND is simplified to NAND).

The same principle applies with more than two inputs. Further, the NAND gate is easily modified to form any of the other logic functions by *negation* or *inversion,* modifying the response. These functions are (still restricting description to two inputs):

AND — output when A *and* B input signals are both present
OR — output when input A *or* B is present

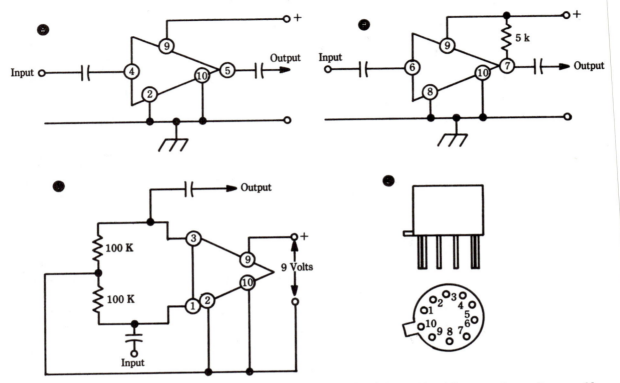

Fig. 13-2. *Three amplifiers based on the CA 3035 IC, all giving a gain of about 100. All external capacitors are 10 microfarad.*

(This is different to a NAND gate, for with no input at A or B there is no output, but with a NAND gate there is output.)

NOR — NOT-OR

Pursuing the subject of logic could fill the rest of the chapter, or even the whole book, so we will get back to digital integrated circuits.

Digital logic ICs are produced in various different families, identified by letters. These letters are an abbreviation of the configuration of the gate circuit employed. The main families are:

- TTL (transistor-transistor logic) — The most popular family with a capability for performing a large number of functions. TTL logic is based on multiple NAND gates.
- DTL (diode-transistor logic) — Another major family, and again based upon multiple NAND gates.
- RTL (resistor-transistor-logic) — Based upon multiple NOR gates which occupy minimum space.
- DCTL (direct-coupled-transistor logic) — Based upon multiple NOR gates similar to RTL but without base resistors.

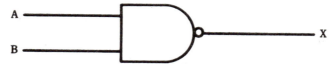

Fig. 13-3. The NAND gate shown in simple diagrammatic form.

- ECL (emitter-coupled logic)—May be based upon multiple OR or NAND gates.
- MOS (metal-oxide-semiconductor logic)—Also called a CMOS since it uses complementary MOS devices. These chips are of LSI construction, with a very high component density. Some 5,000 MOS devices can be accommodated in a chip about 0.15 in. cube. CMOS is usually based upon multiple NAND gate logic.

Regardless of the family used, the basic AND, OR, NAND and NOR gates are combined in one integrated chip of the same family in various combinations of gates and flip-flops to perform specific circuit functions. These functions may or may not be compatible with other families (e.g., TTL functions are compatible with DTL). Also there may be direct equivalents of the complete chip in different families (e.g., TTL, DTL and CMOS). Family development continues and more and more functions are continually appearing, performed by yet more and more ICs appearing on the market.

The computer is a digital logic system. A computer consists of four basic parts:

- The input section
- The CPU (central processing unit)
- The memory
- The output

In order for a digital system to be called a computer, it must meet five essential criteria:

- It must have input capability
- It must have memory to store data.
- It must be capable of making calculations.
- It must be capable of making decisions.
- It must have output capability.

A block diagram of a computer is shown in Fig. 13-4. The input section accepts information from a selected input device and converts it into digital information, which can be understood by the central processing unit. The CPU controls the timing and data selection points involved with accepting inputs and providing outputs by means of the input/output address bus. The CPU also performs all of the arithmetic calculations and memory storage/retrieval operations. The memory address bus defines a specific area in the memory to be worked upon, and the memory data bus either stores or retrieves data from that specific location. The output section accepts the digital information from the CPU, converts the information into a usable form, and routes it to the appropriate output device.

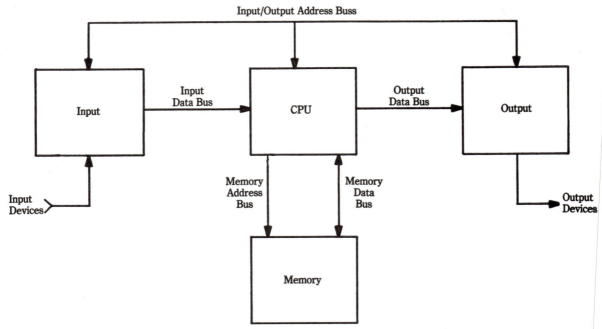

Fig. 13-4. Block diagram illustrating the basic operation of a computer.

The central processing unit (CPU) of a computer can be further divided into the arithmetic logic unit (ALU) and the read only memory (ROM). The ALU controls the logical steps and order for performing arithmetic functions. It interacts with the ROM for instructions for performing redundant operations. The ROM also contains instructions pertaining to start-up and power loss conditions, and instructions for conversion of higher-level languages to machine-language programs (MLP). The CPU usually contains the real time clock (RTC). The RTC is used to cycle the CPU and time the real-time programs as written by the user.

The popularity and success of the computer is governed by the speed of its operations, not the operation complexity. Basically, a computer is only capable of adding, subtracting, and accumulating data. Because it is capable of performing these simple operations at amazingly high speeds, complex mathematical calculations can be broken down into simple steps which the computer can then calculate. For example, a computer actually multiplies by redundant addition of the same number. Division is accomplished by redundant subtraction.

The smallest single operation performed by a computer is the machine cycle. This consists of two stages: the fetch cycle and the execute cycle. During the fetch cycle, the processor fetches an instruction from memory. Then, during the execute cycle, the computer performs some action based upon the content of that instruction. The processor knows which instruction to go to next from the address stored in the program counter. It always contains the address of the next instruction. When program instructions are written, they are arranged in a sequential order, and the program counter simply increments by one for each machine cycle.

If the central processing unit is contained in a single integrated circuit, the IC is referred to as a microprocessor. A computer based on a microprocessor chip is called a microcomputer.

COMPUTER CONTROL OF ANALOG SIGNALS

When a computer needs to examine a continuously variable signal (referred to as an analog signal), the analog signal must be converted to a digital word before the computer can understand it. A logic system designed to do this is called an analog-to-digital converter (commonly symbolized by A/D). If, for example, you want the computer to store an analog voltage level of +16.78 volts, the A/D converter would convert that voltage level to a digital word of 0010100100011011. The numerous 0's and 1's are called *bits* and the entire word is called a *byte*. This one word, or byte, represents the +16.78 voltage level to the computer.

To reconstruct the original analog signal, or any analog signal, a digital-to-analog converter (symbolized by D/A) is required. The D/A converts digital words from the computer to analog voltages and outputs them at the rate at which they were originally collected by the A/D. In this manner, a computer may read or output any analog signal. Most importantly, it can also analyze and manipulate analog signals in the same manner.

14
IC Arrays

IC chips can be divided broadly into two main categories—complete circuits or subcircuits with internal connections, and *arrays*. The latter consist of a number of individual components connected only to the external pins of the IC chips, or, in some cases, two (or possibly more) internally connected components together with individual components. For example, Darlington pairs of transistors included in an array would be connected within the chip.

An example of a simple IC array is shown in Fig. 14-1. It consists of three transistors (two interconnected), two types of diodes, and a Zener diode.

Circuits are commonly designed around IC arrays, in this case, a voltage regulator using two of the transistors, the SCR diode, and the Zener diode. This circuit design is shown in Fig. 14-2. The components to be utilized which are contained in the IC are enclosed in the dashed outline, Q2, Q3, SCR, and Z1. The other components in the chip (Q1 and Q4) are not required. Resistors R1, R2, R3, and R4 and a capacitor C, are all discrete components connected externally.

Figure 14-3 shows this circuit redrawn as a physical diagram, relating the connection of external components to the chip. Pins in this diagram are shown in the actual physical order they appear on the integrated circuit. For ease of reading, pins are shown numbered and enclosed in circles rather than numbered tags. On circuit drawings, pin numbers may be shown circled or not. For clarity, the integrated circuit is drawn much larger in proportion to the external components.

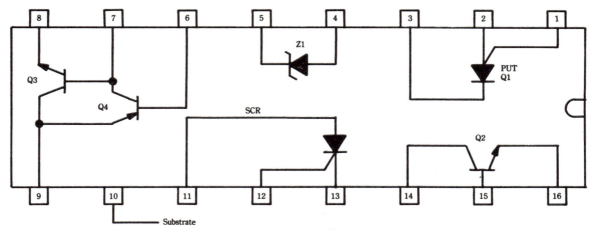

Fig. 14-1. CA3907E (SK3616) IC array schematic.

Connections for completing the circuit of Fig. 14-3 are:

- Leads 1, 2, and 3 are ignored as Q1 is not used.
- Lead 4 connects one side of the Zener diode to the common ground line.
- Lead 5 to Lead 13, connects the Zener diode to the correct side of the SCR.
- Leads 11 and 12 connect together (the SCR is used as a simple diode in this circuit, and the gate connection is not required).

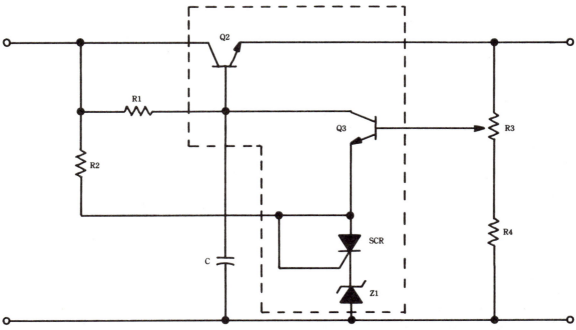

Fig. 14-2. Voltage regulator circuit using CA3097 (SK3613) array.

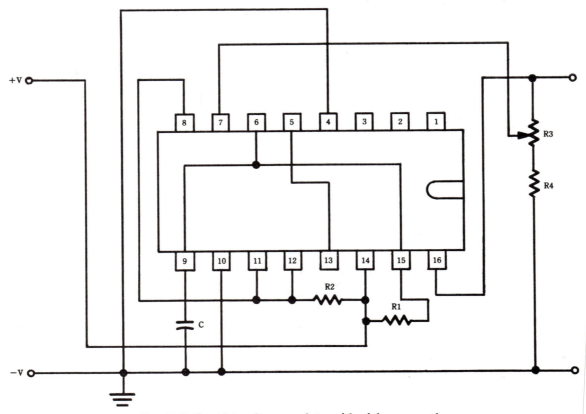

Fig. 14-3. Complete voltage regulator with wiring connections.

Now to pick up the transistor connections; The base of Q2 (15) connects to the external resistor R1, and the collector lead (14) to the other side of R1, which is also the input point for the circuit. The emitter lead (16) connects to output.

Q3 and Q4 in the chip are interconnected, but only one of these transistors is required. Connecting lead (6) to (9) shorts out Q4, which is not wanted. Connecting the emitter lead (8) of Q3 to 11 – 12 (already joined), the collector lead (9) to (6), and the base lead (7) to the center tap of the external potentiometer R3 connects Q3 into the circuit.

It only remains for the external component connections to be completed. These are:

- R2 to lead (14) and lead (12).
- Capacitor C to lead (6) and ground point. Lead (10) on the IC is also the substrate or ground point of the IC, so should also be connected to the common ground line.
- One end of the potentiometer R3 to the top (output) line.
- The other end of the potentiometer to R4.
- The other end of R4 to the bottom common ground line.

You'll notice from this circuit, and a study of others, that the number of components in an array may not be used in a particular circuit, but the cost of the single IC can often be less than that of the equivalent transistors or diodes ordered separately and used individually to complete the same circuit. A circuit using the IC is also more compact and generally easier to construct.

A little study sometimes shows where further savings are possible. Figure 14-5 for example, shows a voltage doubler circuit for a 1-kHz square-wave input signal, based on a CA3096E IC array Fig. 14-5 which contains 5 transistors. Only three of these transistors are used in this particular circuit, leaving two spare.

The circuit calls for two diodes, D1 and D2 (as well as three resistors and two capacitors), to be added as discrete components. Transistors can also be used as diodes (by neglecting the collector lead), and so the functions of D1 and D2 could be performed by the two "spare" transistors in the array (thus using up all its components).

Alternatively, since the current needs a square wave input signal, the two spare transistors could be used in a multivibrator circuit to provide this input, in this case using discrete components for D1 and D2. Since diodes are cheaper than transistors, this is a more economic way of using all the components in the original array.

The fact that popular ICs are quite cheap means that is seldom worthwhile going to elaborate methods of trying to use all the components available in an array, unless such utilization is fairly obvious, as above. Using only part of an array can still show savings over the purchase of individual components for many circuits.

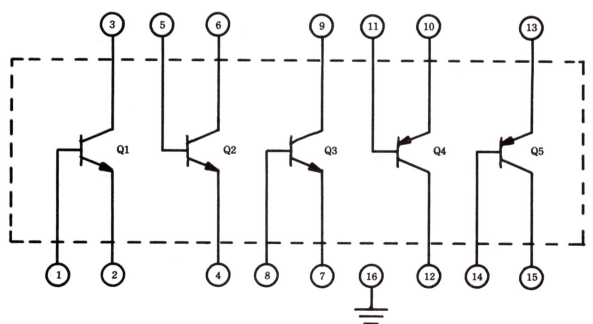

Fig. 14-4. Schematic diagram of CA3600 (SK9205) array.

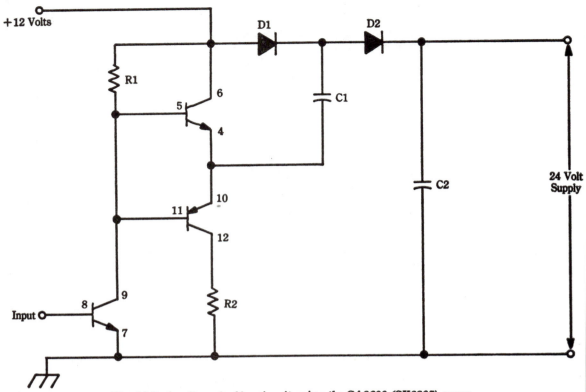

Fig. 14-5. *A voltage doubler circuit using the CA3600 (SK9205)* **array.**

Component values for Fig. 14-4 are:

R1 = 10 ohms
R2 = 1 k
C1 = 2.5 μF
C2 = 2.5 μF
Diodes D1 and D2

15
Transistor Characteristics

A transistor is a three-electrode device, the connections being to *base* (designated B or b), *emitter* (designated E or e), and *collector* (designated C or c). Invariably (except when a transistor is being used as a diode), one electrode is common to both input and output circuits — usually the emitter (common emitter), or sometimes the base (common base). The common-collector configuration is seldom used.

DC PARAMETERS

The four main parameters governing the dc performance of a transistor are:

- input voltage
- input current
- output voltage
- output current

Capital letters are used to designate average voltages and currents, and lower-case letters to designate instantaneous volumes of voltage or current:

- V for average voltages
- v for instantaneous voltages
- I for average currents
- i for instantaneous currents

For example: V_B, V_c, V_e means average values of base, collector, and emitter currents respectively, and v_b, v_c, v_e means instantaneous values of base, collector, and emitter current, respectively. I_B, I_c, I_e means average values of base, collector, and emitter currents, respectively, and i_b, i_c, i_e means instantaneous values of base, collector, and emitter currents respectively.

Where instantaneous *total* values of voltage or current are referred to, a capital subscript is used, with a lowercase letter designating voltage or current. Thus v_B, v_C, v_E mean instantaneous total values of base, collector and emitter voltage respectively, or i_B, i_C, i_E mean instantaneous total values of base, collector and emitter current respectively.

It is also necessary to define the electrodes between which these voltages or currents apply. This is done by using the appropriate letters in the subscript:

V_{BE} = average base-emitter voltage
v_{be} = instantaneous base-emitter voltage
v_{BE} = instantaneous total base emitter voltage
V_{CE} = average collector-emitter voltage
V_{ce} = instantaneous collector-emitter voltage
v_{CE} = instantaneous total collector-emitter voltage
V_{BC} = average base-collector voltage
v_{be} = instantaneous base-collector voltage
v_{BC} = instantaneous total base-collector voltage

Logically, these should conform to the voltage direction (positive to negative), depending on whether the transistor is a PNP or NPN type, as in the following order:

PNP transistor = EB, BC, BE (or eb, bc, be)
NPN transistor = BE, CB, EB (or be, cb, eb)

INPUT CHARACTERISTICS

The input characteristics of a transistor show the variation of input current with input voltage. In the common-emitter configuration, input is to the base, and base current (I_b) is plotted against the base voltage measured between the base and emitter (V_{be}). In the common-base configuration, input is to the emitter, so the input characteristics show the variation of emitter current (I_e) against emitter voltage measured between emitter and base (V_{eb}).

These relationships are given graphically in Fig. 15-1. The input resistance in each case is the reciprocal of the slope of the curve and is therefore low. Because the input characteristics are non-linear (shown by a curve rather than a straight line), input resistance is not constant but depends on the current at which it is measured. Because of the non-linear characteristics of the input, a transistor is normally current biased and driven from a current rather than a voltage source. This is provided by using an effective source resistance which is large in comparison with the input resistance. If this resistance (or, correctly speaking, impedance) is not high enough to swamp the varying resistance (impedance) of the transistor under drive, there will be considerable distortion of the input signal.

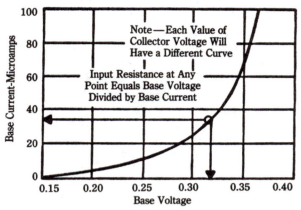

Fig. 15-1. *Typical transistor input characteristics.*

TRANSFER CHARACTERISTICS

Transfer characteristics of a transistor are normally given as a plot of collector current against base current, Fig. 15-2. Ideally, this should be a straight line. Any departure from a linear (straight line) relationship implies non-linear distortion of the output signal.

OUTPUT CHARACTERISTICS

Output characteristic curves of a transistor show what is effectively a switch-on voltage (or *knee voltage* as it is called), above which a large change in collector voltage produces only a small change in collector current. Since resistance is again the reciprocal of the slope of this I_c/V_c curve, it follows that output

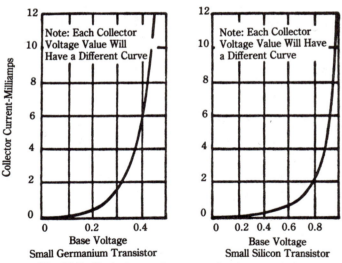

Fig. 15-2. *Typical transistor transfer characteristics.*

resistance of a transistor is characteristically high. The value of the collector current, and to some extent the slope of the curve, also depends on the base current. Separate curves are thus plotted for (constant) base currents, see Fig. 15-3. Again, note that a constant base current is only obtained with a high source resistance in the base circuit. Also, any non-linearity in the transfer characteristics of the transistor shows up on the input characteristics as uneven spacing of the curves for equal increments in input current.

CURRENT AMPLIFICATION

A transistor is generally used as a current amplifier. Here, the base current controls the current in the emitter-collector circuit, although it may only be a small percentage of the emitter current. Current can be added in the usual way. Thus, emitter current equals collector current plus base current; or, alternatively, base current equals emitter current minus collector current.

In expressing the characteristics of the transistor, collector current divided by emitter current is designated α, and collector current divided by base current is designated α^1. Knowing either α or α^1, it is possible to find the currents at the other electrodes since

$$\alpha = \alpha^1/(1 + \alpha^1)$$
$$\alpha^1 = \alpha/(1 - \alpha)$$

Actual values of α and α^1 can vary with frequency and current for the same transistor. Straightforward, simple, analysis of transistor characteristics is based on low signal currents at zero frequency; i.e., small changes in direct current. To

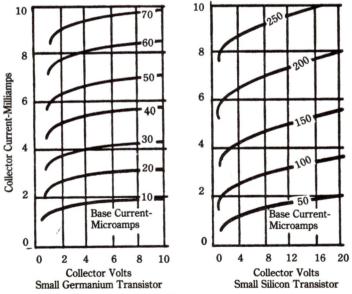

Fig. 15-3. *Typical transistor output characteristics.*

make this clear, the symbols α_o and $\alpha_o{}^1$ are sometimes used, the subscript "o" indicating zero frequency.

The *current amplification factor* in common-emitter configuration (input to the base) is given by α^1 (or $\alpha_o{}^1$). It is largely independent of collector voltage, but is usually measured at some constant collector voltage. Specifically, the value of α^1 is directly related to the slope of the I_e/I_b curve, or the transfer characteristics. It is also called the *small-signal gain* of the transistor. Actual values may range from as low as 10 up to several hundreds.

In the common-base configuration, with input to emitter, the current amplification factor is designated α (or α_o) and is equivalent to the slope of the I_c/I_e curve. In this case, I_c is always a little less than I_e, so the value of α is always less than unity; typically of the order of 0.98.

DC CURRENT GAIN

Specifically, this is the ratio of I_c/I_b in common-emitter configuration and is generally referred to as β (strictly speaking β') or h_{FE}, the latter normally being the parameter quoted by manufacturers. β and h_{FE} are not identical, and both vary with collector current. The quoted h_{FE} value is therefore normally associated with a specific collector current. Commonly available transistors may have values of h_{FE} varying from about 10 to 560 at collector currents ranging from 1 mA to 30 A. Here are some examples:

- Low and medium power germanium transistors: typical h_{FE} range 30 – 200 at collector currents from 1 mA to 300 mA
- Small signal high frequency germanium transistors: typical h_{FE} range 30 – 100 at collector currents from 1 mA to 10 mA
- Germanium power transistors: typical h_{FE} range 40 – 150 at collector currents from 500 mA to 1A
- Small signal silicon transistors: typical f_{FE} range 50 – 500 at collector currents from 0.1 mA to 50 mA
- Medium power low frequency silicon transistors: typical h_{FE} range 90 – 200 at collector currents from 10 mA to 150 mA
- High power low frequency silicon transistors: typical h_{FE} range 25 – 100 at collector currents from 150 mA to 5 A
- Small signal high frequency silicon transistors: typical h_{FE} range 40 – 100 and collector currents from 1 mA to 25 mA

MANUFACTURER'S SPECIFICATIONS

Manufacturers' normally provide curves showing the static (dc) characteristics of industrial transistors for both common emitter and common base configurations, together with other characteristic values as appropriate. Summarized transistor data in catalogs or data sheets should give at least the following:

$$V_{CEO} \text{ (max)} = \text{maximum collector to emitter}$$
$$\text{voltage on open current}$$

$$V_{CBO} \text{ (max)} = \text{maximum collector to base}$$
$$\text{voltage on open current}$$
$$V_{EBO} \text{ (max)} = \text{maximum emitter to base}$$
$$\text{voltage on open current}$$
$$I_c \text{ (max)} = \text{maximum collector current}$$
$$P_t \text{ (max) or } P_{tot} \text{ (max)} = \text{maximum total power dissipation}$$
$$h_{FE} = \text{dc current gain (usually quoted}$$
$$\text{as a typical figure at a specific}$$
$$\text{collector current)}$$

To assist selection, such listings may be arranged in groups of (roughly) similar types. It is even more helpful when the design application is also shown for each transistor type, such as general purpose, switching, audio amp, etc. Here is a useful classification and guide.

Germanium Transistors

- Small, medium-current, switching and general purpose
- Medium-current switching, low power output
- Small, medium-current amplifiers
- AF amplifiers, low power output
- Complementary pairs
- High power output (power transistor)

Silicon Transistors

- AF amplifiers, small signal, general purpose
- AF amplifiers, low level, low noise
- Small-signal amplifiers
- RF amplifiers and oscillators
- Medium-current switching, low power output
- High frequency, medium powers
- General-purpose switching
- Power transistors

Any reference to power grouping is largely arbitrary since there is no universal agreement on the range of power levels (referring to the maximum power rating of the particular transistor). Thus, low power may generally be taken to cover 100–250 mW, but such a grouping may include transistors with power ratings up to 1 watt. Similarly, medium power implies a possible power range of 250 mW to 1 W, but may extend up to 5 watts. Any transistor with a power rating of greater than 5 watts is classified as a power transistor. Information about selecting transistors for characteristics is given in the next chapter.

BASIC GUIDE TO SELECTING TRANSISTORS

Transistors are specified by code letters and/or numbers, by the manufacturers. Published circuit designs normally specify a particular type of transistor, all the associated component values—such as resistors—then being determined with respect to the characteristics of the particular transistor specified. No problem there. Simply use the specified transistor—unless, as can happen, you find that it is unobtainable.

In that case, there are basically three options. The first is to use an *equivalent* transistor, of different manufacture or type number, which has the same characteristics. For this you need a history of transistor equivalents from which to select an alternative. There are books available which give such equivalent listings, or your local hobby shop or parts distributor may be able to help.

Equivalents given in such listings are seldom exact equivalents. They are more likely to be near-equivalent with sufficiently close characteristics to be used in basic circuits where component values are not too critical. Simple radio circuits are an example. In many cases with elementary circuits, almost any type of transistor of the same basic type (germanium or silicon), or better still, the same functional group, will work.

Information on functional grouping is harder to come by. Manufacturers group their products in this way, but suppliers usually only list their stocks by type number, which is not very helpful without manufacturers' catalogs to check on the functional group to which a particular transistor conforms. When you can find transistor types listed under functional groups, keep this material on file. It can be an invaluable guide in selecting transistors for a particular job.

IDENTIFYING TRANSISTORS BY SHAPE

While transistors are made in thousands of different types, the number of shapes in which they are produced is more limited and more or less standardized in a simple code: TO (Transistor Outline) followed by a number.

TO1 is the original transistor shape—a cylindrical can with the three leads emerging in triangular pattern from the bottom. Looking at the bottom, the upper lead in the triangle is the *base,* the one to the right (marked by a color spot) the *collector,* and the one to the left the *emitter.* The collector lead may also be more widely spaced from the base lead than is the emitter lead.

In other TO shapes, the three leads may emerge in similar triangular pattern (but not necessarily with the same positions for base, collector, and emitter), or in-line. Just to confuse the issue, there are also sub-types of the same TO number shapes with different lead designations. The TO92, for example, has three leads emerging in line parallel to a flat side, or an otherwise circular can, reading 1, 2, 3 from top to bottom, with the flat side to the right (looking at the bottom).

To complicate things further, some transistors may have only two emerging leads (the third connected to the case internally), and some transistor outline shapes are found with more than three leads emerging from the base. These, in fact, are integrated circuits (ICs), packaged in the same outline shape as a transistor. More complex ICs are packaged in quite different form.

Power transistors are easily identified by shape. They are metal cased with an elongated bottom and two mounting holes. In this case, there are only two leads — the emitter and base — and these are normally marked. The collector is connected internally to the can, and so connection to the collector is via one of the mounting bolts or bottom of the can.

Examples of transistor outline shapes together with typical dimensions and lead identification are given in Fig. 9-10.

16
Amplifiers

An amplifier can be defined as a device or circuit providing multiplication of a signal; i.e., an output signal greater than the input signal.

Transistors work as an amplifier of signals. In the most widely used mode of connection of transistors for such duties, with input and output circuits both connected to the emitter (common-emitter mode), the degree of amplification or current gain is called the *beta* (β) of the transistor.

BASIC AMPLIFIER CIRCUITS

A basic transistor amplifier circuit is very simple, and is identical for a PNP or NPN transistor, except for the battery polarity (Fig. 16-1). Virtually any low-power af transistor can be used in this circuit. The bias resistor (R) must have a value providing a collector current not exceeding the maximum specified rating for the transistor used, the actual current flowing in the collector circuit also being influenced by the voltage of the battery.

Knowing the transistor characteristics, a suitable value for R in Fig. 16-1 can be calculated as follows:

$$R = \text{gain} \times \frac{\text{battery voltage}}{\text{collector current}}$$

$$= h_{FE} \times \frac{\text{battery voltage}}{I_c}$$

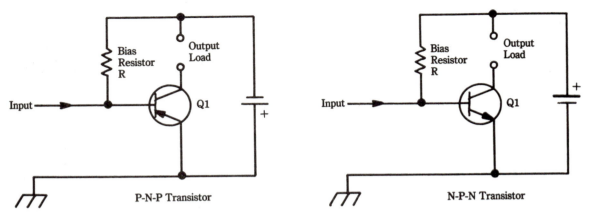

Fig. 16-1. Basic amplifier circuit.

where I_c is equal to, or preferably less than, the specification figure for I_c max. For example, a small signal transistor has the values of I_c max = 250 mA, and h_{FE} = 30 to 90. Taking the maximum gain, and 175 mA as a safe working figure for the collector current:

$$R = 90 \times \frac{9}{0.175}$$

$$= 4,630 \ \Omega$$

A suitable (preferred-value) resistor would thus be 4.7 k.

Figure 16-2 shows the complete circuit for an elementary af amplifier of this type, coupled to the front end of a basic crystal set. The detector (output) is coupled to the amplifier via capacitor C2, a suitable value for which would be 10 μF or higher (20, 25, 30, 40, or 50 μF): Capacitor C1 (0.001 μF) may not be necessary. The output load in the collector circuit is formed by high-impedance phones.

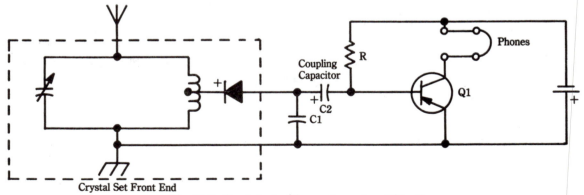

Fig. 16-2. Crystal set with one stage of amplification.

Note that the *polarity* of the battery used to power this circuit is important as far as the transistor connections is concerned and also because of the connections to the diode and C2 (which normally needs to be an electrolytic type to provide the high-capacitance value required). With an NPN transistor, the battery polarity is reversed, as are the diode and electrolytic-capacitor connections.

The same type of circuit can be used to provide additional amplification simply by adding another amplifier stage (Fig. 17-3). The second amplifier stage can be identical to the first, or based on a higher-power transistor taking the output present and providing even greater gain. The load in the output (collector) of the first amplifier stage is provided by a resistor (R2) (which should be about the same value as the phone resistance, 3.3 to 4.7 k). The two stages are coupled by a capacitor (C3). The value of R3 depends on the second transistor used, and may be anything from 130 to 1 k Ω. Capacitors C2 and C3 can be 10 μF or larger.

A more compact two-stage amplifier circuit is shown in Fig. 17-4. This may prove capable of operating a small loudspeaker direct, although the current drain is quite high.

Alternatively, three or four stages of amplification using low-power transistors, following a basic front end crystal set, should provide enough power to drive a small loudspeaker at the final output, through a suitable step-down transformer to provide an impedance match.

Simple amplifier circuits of this type have an important limitation: performance of the transistor(s) tends to vary with temperature. There is also the possibility of thermal runaway developing, which can destroy the transistors, because, as the external temperature increases the collector current also tends to increase, which in turn causes a further increase in junction temperature. The effect is cumulative and goes from bad to worse, even to the point of ruining the transistor completely. It is possible to overcome this trouble by arranging for the circuit to be self-biasing or dc stabilized so that a constant collector current is

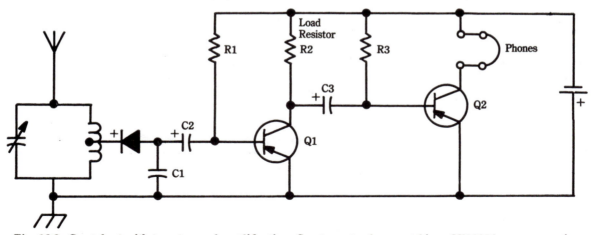

Fig. 16-3. Crystal set with two stages of amplification. Component values matching SK3007A or near equivalent for Q1 and Q2.

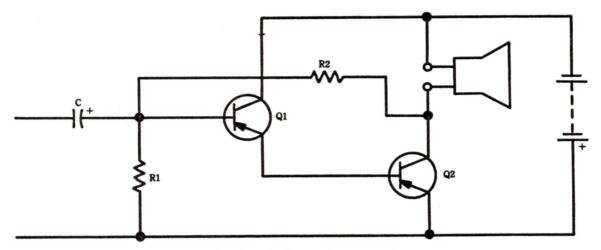

Fig. 16-4. Amplifier for loudspeaker output. Components:

Q1 = SK3004   R1 = 6.8k
Q2 = SK3014   R2 = 33k
C8 = 10 microfarads

provided, regardless of transistor type or temperature variations. In other words, the working point of the collector circuit is stabilized.

A further advantage of a stabilized circuit is that it makes the performance of the amplifier less dependent on the characteristics of individual transistors, which can differ appreciably even for the same type. Capacitor-coupling between stages should be used, since this makes each stage independent, rather than interdependent.

To achieve this, the original bias resistor is split into two separate values, R1 and R2 (Fig. 16-5). A further bias resistor (R3) is applied directly to the emitter, in parallel with a capacitor (C) to act as a bypass for af currents.

A receiver design incorporating two stages of amplification with stabilized circuits, following a conventional front end is shown in Fig. 16-6. This, in fact, is about as far as it is practical to go with such a basic circuit because, although additional complete stages provide more gain and greater final output power, any deficiency in the circuit is also aggravated—notably, lack of sensitivity and selectivity in the front end.

The amplifier stages also provide a convenient point to insert a volume control into the receiver circuit. This takes the form of a potentiometer which can replace one of the bias resistors, or be placed in series with the flow of the current after the first stage of amplification (Fig. 16-7). This introduces minimum distortion over the volume control range.

Amplifier Output Stages

Single transistor outputs work in Class-A operation, which means that the values of bias and signal voltage applied to the transistor ensure that collector

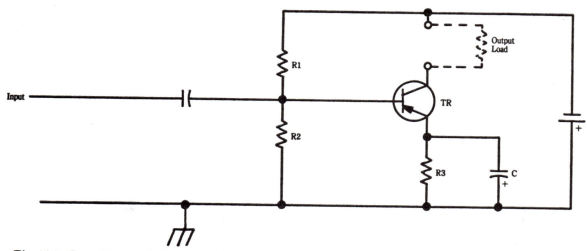

Fig. 16-5. Transistor amplifier stage with stabilized bias. Typical values for low/medium power transistors:

$$R1 = 22k$$
$$R2 = 10k$$
$$R3 = 1k$$
$$C = 10\ microfarads$$

current always flows. Figure 16-8 shows a basic Class-A output circuit incorporating transformer coupling to a loudspeaker.

A more economic way of producing satisfactory output power is to use a single transistor driver working a complementary pair of transistors (an NPN and a PNP selected with matched characteristics) in push-pull configuration. The out-

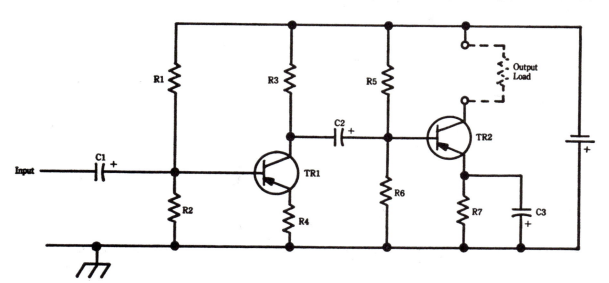

Fig. 16-6. Two stage amplifier circuit.

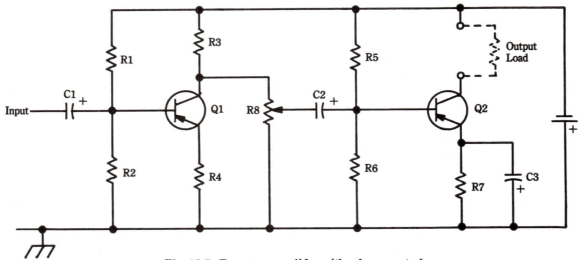

Fig. 16-7. *Two stage amplifier with volume control.*

put power obtained from a pair of transistors in push-pull is considerably more than double the power obtained from a single transistor of the same type.

With Class B operation, the transistors are biased to nearly cut-off, so that only a marginal current flows under quiet conditions. Push-pull outputs may, however, also be designed for Class AB operation, with rather higher current drains.

Basically, distortion is lowest with Class A operation, while Class B operation provides the lowest current drain but introduces the possibility of crossover distortion being present. This can be overcome by applying a slight forward bias to each transistor. Class AB offers a compromise between the two.

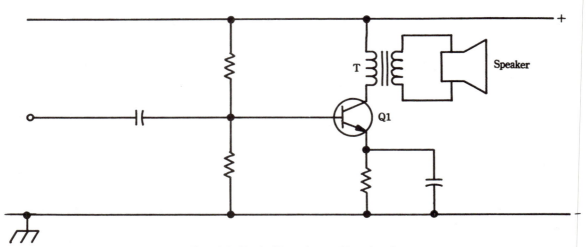

Fig. 16-8. *Basic Class A amplifier circuit.*

Two types of basic push-pull output circuits are shown in Figs. 16-9 and 16-10, one with direct coupling and the other using transformer coupling, both interstage (between driver and push-pull input) and to the loudspeaker. The coupling transformer can provide voltage step-up. An output transformer, on the other hand, is invariably a step-down type to adjust the loudspeaker impedance to the required output impedance. Both types of circuits have their advantages and disadvantages, although for simpler receivers, all-transistor circuits are usually preferred.

Much also depends on the requirements of the receiver. To operate a small loudspeaker successfully, an audio power output of 5 mA or better is required (higher still for larger speakers, of course). At the other extreme, about 10 μA represents, for most people, the threshold of audibility in high-impedance phones; and 0.1 mA is a normal minimum for comfortable listening and ready identification of sounds in headphones. For easy listening with high-impedance phones, an audio output power of up to 0.5 mA is desirable. Higher signal levels tend to swamp headphones but can, of course, be reduced by a volume control.

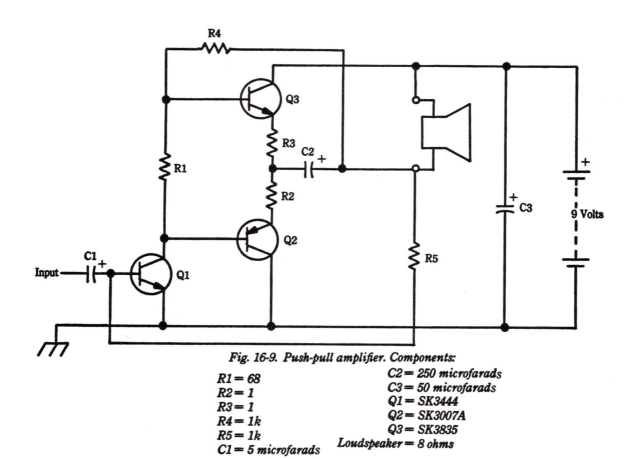

Fig. 16-9. Push-pull amplifier. Components:

R1 = 68
R2 = 1
R3 = 1
R4 = 1k
R5 = 1k
C1 = 5 microfarads
C2 = 250 microfarads
C3 = 50 microfarads
Q1 = SK3444
Q2 = SK3007A
Q3 = SK3835
Loudspeaker = 8 ohms

117

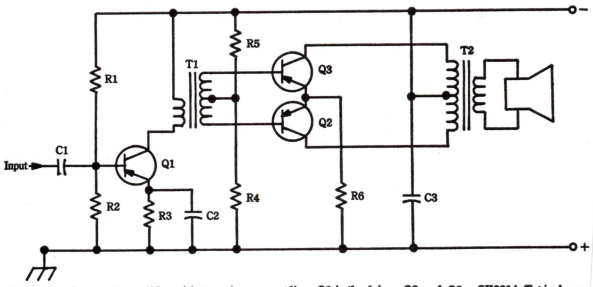

Fig. 16-10. Push-pull amplifier with transformer coupling. Q1 is the driver; Q2 and Q3 = SK3014. Typical component values:

R1, R2 = to match Q1 (depending on type used)	
R3 = 1k	C2 = 50 microfarads
R4 = 100	C3 = 50 microfarads
R5 = 4.7k	T1 = coupling transformer
R6 = 10	T2 = output transformer

Typical characteristics of headphones, earpieces, and loudspeakers are listed here.

Headphones

- High-impedance type: dc resistance 2,000–4,000 ohms, typical impedance 10,000 ohms (at 1 kHz)
- Low-impedance type: dc resistance 15 ohms, typical impedance 80 ohms (at 1 kHz)
- Low impedance type: dc resistance 80 ohms, typical impedance 120 ohms (at 1 kHz)

Earpieces

- High-impedance type: dc resistance 2,000 ohms, typical impedance 15 ohms (at 1 kHz)

- High impedance type: dc resistance 14 ohms, typical impedance 60 ohms (at 1 kHz)

- High impedance type: dc resistance 60 ohms, typical impedance 250 ohms (at 1 kHz)

Loudspeakers

Typical dc resistance 3 ohms, typical impedance 8–16 ohms.

Step-Down Transformers

It is obvious from a study of these figures that low-impedance phones, a low-impedance earpiece, or a loudspeaker will be a mismatch for coupling to an output requiring a high-impedance load (as in the case of most of the simple all-transistor output circuits).

To employ low-impedance phones, earpiece, or a loudspeaker with an output requiring a high-impedance load, a matching step-down transformer (output transformer) must be used. The primary of the transformer then provides the required output load, indirecly coupled to the secondary to which is connected the low-impedance phones or speaker, Fig. 16-11. The turns ratio required from the transformer is easily calculated as:

$$\sqrt{\left(\frac{\text{output load impedance required in ohms}}{\text{phone or speaker impedance in ohms}}\right)}$$

Some typical transformer ratios and their suitability for matching are:

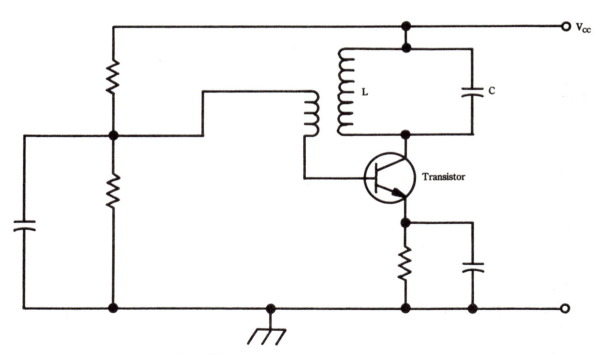

Fig. 16-11. Using an output transformer to balance the load.

119

Ratio	Listening Device	Equivalent Output Load Impedance Ohms
41:1	Speaker	29,000
35:1	4-ohm earpiece	20,000
30:1	Speaker	10,000
18:1	14-ohm earpiece	20,000
14:1	15-ohm earpiece	20,000
9:1	60-ohm earpiece	20,000
5:1	80-ohm headphones	20,000

17
Oscillators

An oscillator can be described in simple terms as an alternating current generator. Where only low frequencies are required, as in mains electricity for example, rotating machines offer a straightforward solution and can also operate at high power levels. In electronic circuits where very much higher ac frequencies are required, these are provided by oscillator circuits. They fall broadly into three types: resonant-frequency oscillators, crystal-controlled oscillators, and phase-shift oscillators.

RESONANT-FREQUENCY OSCILLATORS

Resonant-frequency oscillator circuits are based on the particular property of an inductance (L) and an associated capacitance (C) to exhibit resonance whereby the current flowing in the circuit oscillates from positive to negative in a sinusoidal manner at a frequency determined only by the values of L and C. Figure 18-1 illustrates such a circuit.

In the initial state, with the switch in position, there is a steady current flowing through the coil but with no appreciable voltage, and so the capacitor remains uncharged. Movement of the switch to position 2 puts a large negative bias on the gate of the FET so that the drain current is cut off. The resultant collapse of magnetic flux in the coil opposes the charge, so that current continues to flow into the capacitor, charging it up. Voltage across the capacitor can only increase at the expense of decreasing current, however, so a point is reached where the current falls to zero and the voltage is a maximum.

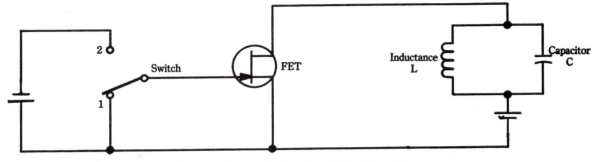

Fig. 17-1. Demonstration circuit for LC oscillator.

At this point, the capacitor starts to discharge, generating a current in the reverse direction, with falling voltage. This continues until the voltage has dropped to zero, corresponding to maximum reverse current. All the energy stored in the LC circuit is now returned to L but with reverse polarity. Consequently, the voltage starts to increase in a negative direction, with the current decreasing, ending up with the capacitor charged in the reverse direction (maximum negative voltage) when the current again reaches zero. The circuit now starts to rise again in a positive direction with falling negative voltage to complete a full cycle of oscillation, as shown in Fig. 18-2. The cycle of operation is repeated over and over again at a frequency given by:

$$\frac{1}{2\pi \times \sqrt{LC}}$$

Theoretically at least, with an ideal inductance and an ideal capacitor, neither having any electrical resistance, the original store of energy is exchanged indefinitely; i.e., oscillation continues indefinitely in a sinusoidal manner with no further energy fed into the circuit (the original source of battery energy is switched off once the switch is moved from position 1 to position 2). In a practical circuit, however, there is some resistance present, which produces a gradual decay or *damping* of the amplitude of the oscillators (i.e., reduction in maximum voltage and current values).

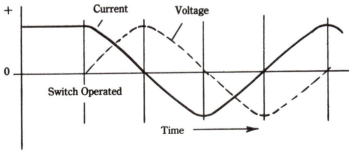

Fig. 17-2. Cycle of operation of LC oscillator.

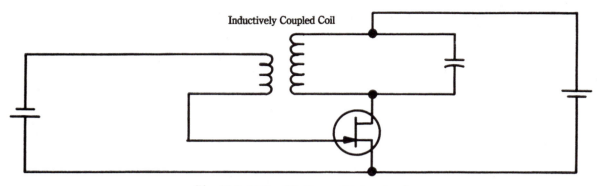

Fig. 17-3. Self-oscillating oscillator circuit.

The degree of damping present is dependent on the ratio of reactance to resistance in the LC circuit, or Q. The lower the value of Q, the greater the damping present. If the Q is as low as 1:2, the circuit is critically damped and does not oscillate at all. In other words, if conditions are right for the LC circuit to start oscillating, this is damped out completely in the first cycle. Equally, the higher the Q, the greater the length of time oscillation continues. However, in a practical oscillator circuit, some energy must be supplied to the circuit to keep it oscillating, to replace the energy dissipated in the resistance present in the circuit. Also, this supply of energy needs to be provided automatically in a practical circuit. Figure 17-3 shows how the original demonstration circuit can be modified to provide just this.

Here, the small coil inductively coupled to L generates a voltage exactly synchronized with the sinusoidal voltage generated in the LC circuit. The value of this voltage depends on the number of turns in the small coil and how closely it is coupled to L. The induced voltage can work with or against the voltage in the LC circuit. In other words, it only works if the coil is connected one way. If the coupling is close, and the coil is connected the right way, such a circuit can be self-oscillating started up by random electron movements.

PRACTICAL LC OSCILLATORS

The basic requirements for a practical resonant-frequency or LC oscillator are thus an oscillatory circuit (L and C), associated with some means of maintaining oscillation (usually some form of amplifier such as a transistor, FET, or op-amp).

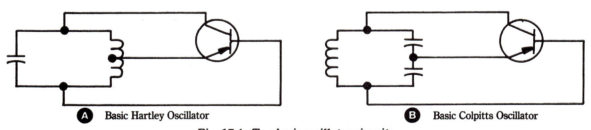

Fig. 17-4. Two basic oscillator circuits.

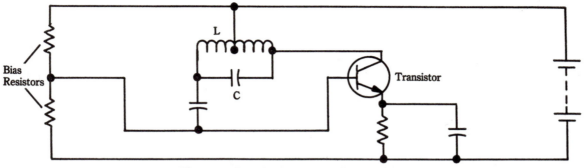

Fig. 17-5. Practical Hartley oscillator circuit.

Two ways of doing this using a transistor as the maintaining amplifier are shown in Fig. 17-4. In the first (A), the LC circuit is tapped on the inductive side. This is the basis of the Hartley oscillator. In the second (B), the LC circuit is tapped on the capacitive side. This is the basis of the Colpitts oscillator. Practical circuits for these two important types of oscillators are shown in Figs. 17-5 and 17-6.

CRYSTAL-CONTROLLED OSCILLATORS

A quartz crystal with electrodes planted on opposite faces, is the electrical equivalent of an inductance (L), resistance (R), and capacitance (C1) in series, with a much larger capacitance (C2) across them, see Fig. 17-7. It is, in fact, a complete LC circuit with a specific resonant frequency which may range from a few kHz to several MHz, depending on the crystal type, size, how it is cut and how it is mounted. It also has the characteristic of a high Q with good stability, making it a most useful device to base an oscillator circuit around. It is also a more or less standard choice for a fixed frequency oscillator.

A whole variety of such circuits are possible. A basic configuration is shown in Fig. 17-8 where the active device is an FET. It should be noted that, although a tuned circuit (LC combination) is included, the oscillator frequency is determined

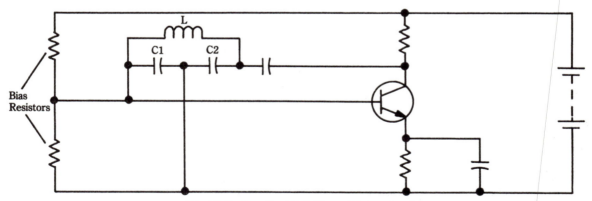

Fig. 17-6. Practical Colpitts oscillator circuit.

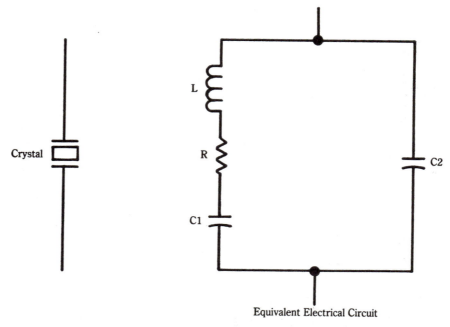

Fig. 17-7. Electrical circuit equivalent of a crystal.

essentially by the resonant frequency of the crystal and not by the rest of the circuit. The tuning of the LC circuit can in fact, be relatively broad around this frequency, the crystal providing stabilized oscillator at a specific frequency.

The frequency of a crystal-controlled oscillator can be adjusted within very narrow limits (usually less than 5 parts in 10,000) by means of a variable capaci-

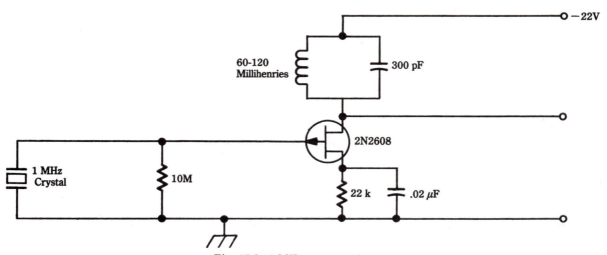

Fig. 17-8. 1 MHz crystal oscillator.

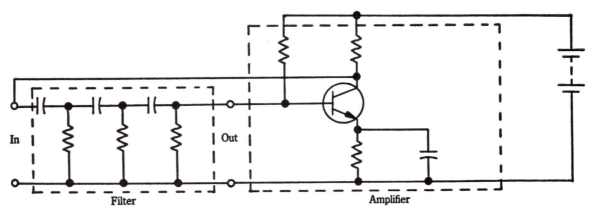

Fig. 17-9. Phase-shift oscillator based on filter circuit.

tor connected across it. However, since crystals are simple, inexpensive devices which can plug into a socket, a change of crystal is usually the easiest method of frequency adjustment.

PHASE-SHIFT OSCILLATORS

It is possible to produce an oscillator on the tuned-circuit principle by employing resistors instead of inductances. Basically, such circuits are filter networks (cascaded RC combinations) associated with an amplifier. A three-stage RC filter circuit is needed to provide a total phase difference of 180 degrees between current and voltage, with a small loss matched by the gain of the amplifier. A basic circuit of this type is shown in Fig. 17-9, using a transistor for the active element. A basic requirement for such a circuit to work is that the input to the amplifier must be at least $1/\beta$ times the output in strength, where β is the gain of the transistor. This generally calls for the use of a transistor with a current gain of the order of 50 or better.

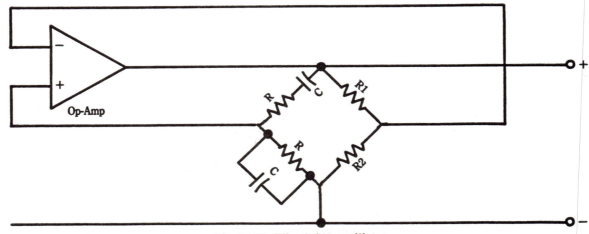

Fig. 17-10. Wien-bridge oscillator.

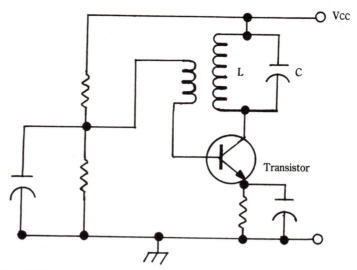

Fig. 17-11. Basic resonant circuit oscillator with transistor amplifier.

A particular advantage of phase-shift oscillators is that they can readily be varied in frequency over a wide range, using three variable capacitors, ganged together and varied simultaneously. Their most useful working range is from a few Hz to hundreds of kHz. At higher frequencies — in the MHz range and above — they are generally inferior to resonant-circuit oscillators.

BRIDGE OSCILLATORS

One other type of oscillator worth describing is the Wien-bridge oscillator (another phase-shift type) where a balanced bridge is used as the feedback network (Fig. 17-10). To work, the loop gain must equal unity and must have zero phase. This is generally given by suitable selection of resistor values so that R2/(R1 + R2) is less than ⅓.

The frequency of operation with this type is the frequency of the balanced bridge, or $\dfrac{1}{2\pi\,RC}$. Note that both the two resistor values and capacitor values on the left-hand side of the bridge are identical. The frequency of the oscillator can be changed by using different values for R, or, alternatively, for a variable-frequency oscillator, the two capacitors are replaced by ganged variable capacitors of identical value, varied simultaneously.

The majority of oscillator circuits, however, are based on resonant circuit or LC combinations of conventional form with a close-coupled second coil to promote self-oscillation. A circuit of this type is shown in Fig. 17-11.

18
Circuit Diagrams

A circuit diagram is a plan of a particular circuit showing all the components and all the circuit connections. The components are represented by symbols (see Chapter 1), arranged to show all connections simply and clearly, avoiding crossing lines as far as possible. It is a theoretical diagram since it does not show the actual size or shape of components, nor their actual position in a built-up circuit. It has to be redrawn as a practical diagram or working plan from which the circuit is actually constructed.

Certain conventions apply in drawing a circuit diagram, but these are not always followed rigidly. The first is that the diagram should read from left to right. That means whatever is input to the circuit should start at the extreme left and be fed through the circuit from left to right. In the simple radio circuit shown in block form in Fig. 18-1 the input is supplied by the antenna current feeding the tuned circuit, then passing to the detector, then to the amplifier, and finally the loudspeaker output. The power supply for the circuit (say a battery) is shown on the far right of the circuit. At first this may seem a contradiction of the rule, if you think of the power supply being put into the circuit. It is not a true input, but is merely a supply to work the circuit. Otherwise it has nothing to do with the circuit, so it is depicted out of the way on the right. There is another good reason for this. Although the supply feeds all the stages backwards in terms of left-to-right reading, it probably is not required to power the first stage. Hence, it is logical to show feed from the right, stopping at the appropriate stage.

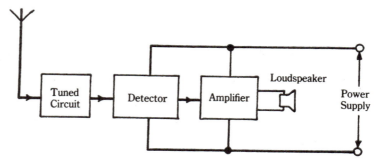

Fig. 18-1. Basic stages in a simple radio receiver.

Nearly all circuits are based on a common line connection; i.e., components in various stages are connected to one side of the supply. This common line is drawn at the bottom of the diagram, as shown in Fig. 18-2. It is generally referred to as the common ground line, although it may not have any actual connection to ground.

A similar common line can also be drawn at the top of the diagram, representing the other side of the supply. Conventionally, this top line is the +, and the bottom or common line the −. This is not always convenient in designing transistor circuits, so this conventional polarity may be reversed on some diagrams.

Working on this basis, and replacing the boxes with individual components, the circuit diagram looks something like Fig. 18-3. Each component is identified by a number, or may have its actual value given alongside. Reading the circuit is fairly straightfoward — with a little practice. Starting from the left, the input from the antenna is fed to L and C1 forming the tuned circuit. From there, it is passed through the diode detector to the amplifier (Q1). Q1 then feeds the final output stage (transistor Q2) driving the loudspeaker. A supply voltage is required only by Q1 and Q2, so the upper common line stops short at Q1 stage. The resistors in the top half regulate the supply; and those in the bottom half (connecting to the common bottom line) establish the working point of the transistors. Additional components (C2 and C3) are required for coupling between stages.

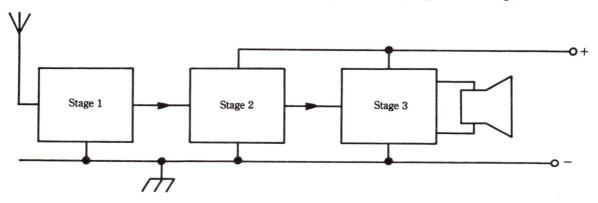

Fig. 18-2. Stages shown with common ground and power supply connections.

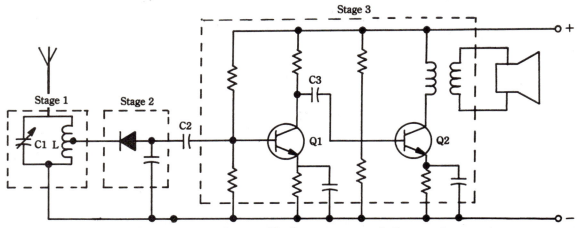

Fig. 18-3. The same stages drawn with all components and all connections required.

Note that all connecting lines meet at right angles, and where such connection occurs, this is further made clear by a ·. If a line on the diagram has to cross another line without any connection to this line, it is simply drawn as a crossing line, as shown in Fig. 18-5 *(right)*. Crossing lines with a · at the point of meeting indicate that all four lines are, in fact, connected at that point. To avoid possible confusion (or accidentally missing the ·), connected lines from each side of another line can be drawn as shown in the right diagram of Fig. 18-4.

So far, there should be no confusion at all in reading theoretical diagrams, but they can become more difficult to follow when the circuit becomes more complex or contains a large number of individual components. One common trick of the trade used to avoid too many crossing lines (which could lead to mistakes in following a particular connection) is to arrow a connecting point, or seprately designate a common line connection (Fig. 18-5). Arrowing is usually applied to outputs, indicating that this line is connected as an input to a separate stage (or even a separate circuit). Showing a separate ground connection is common with components connected between the top line and bottom line. It indicates clearly that the component is to be connected to the ground line, and avoids having to draw this line in close proximity to other components or crossing other lines.

What is less easy to read in terms of actual connections is a circuit incorporating a single physical component which may perform two (or more) separate

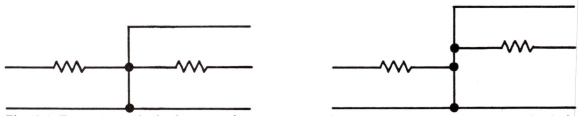

Fig. 18-4. Two methods of indicating connection to a common point. That on the right is often preferred for clarity.

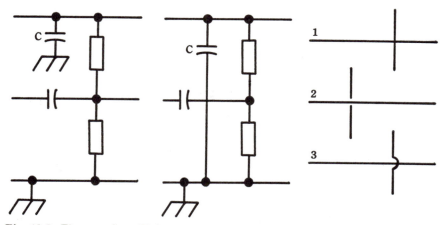

Fig. 18-5. The capacitor (C) is connected between top and bottom lines, but may be shown in a circuit diagram in either of these two ways. On the right are three ways of drawing crossing lines with no connection. Method 1 is the usual way; method 2 is clearer still.

functions. As a very simple example, a volume control potentiometer for a radio may also incorporate on-off switching. The two *functional* features of this single component may appear in quite separate parts of the circuit; e.g., the volume control prior to an amplifier stage and the switch function in the supply line at the far right (Fig. 18-6).

This can be even more confusing at first where a ganged tuning capacitor or a ganged switch is involved, with its separate sections appearing in different parts of the circuit, although it is actually a single physical component. This is the logical — and by far the simplest — way of showing the theoretical connections of the circuit, but when it comes to actual construction of the circuit, connections from two or more different parts of the circuit have to be taken to one particular component position.

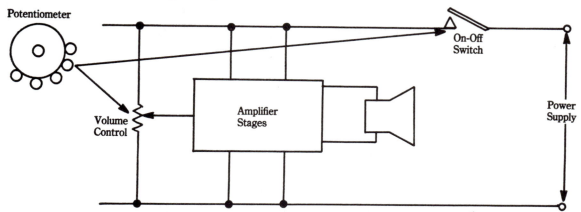

Fig. 18-6. In this example, a single component (the potentiometer connections) appears in two separate parts of the circuit diagram.

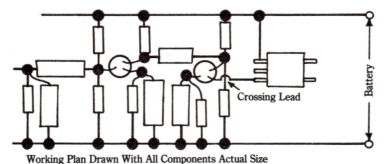

Working Plan Drawn With All Components Actual Size

Fig. 18-7. Typical component layout drawing or working plan. This is the same circuit as Fig. 18-3, following the tuned circuit (which would be a ferrite rod aerial.

As far as possible, actual physical layout of components should follow the same flow path positions as in the theoretical circuit diagram, adjusted as necessary to get components into suitable positions for making connections. Exceptions must arise, particularly as noted above. Just as a theoretical diagram is designed to present the circuit in as simple a manner as possible with all theoretical connections clear, the working circuit must also be planned to be as neat and simple as possible and also as logical as possible as far as placement of components is concerned. It should be prepared as a complete wiring diagram, when it becomes a working plan. Almost inevitably, it will look more confused than the theoretical diagram, with probably a fair number of crossing wires (unless it is planned as a printed circuit — see Chapter 20) and leads running in various directions. Common connecting points are still indicated by a ·, but crossing leads are better shown as definite cross-overs, as in Fig. 18-7. Then there is less risk of wondering whether or not a · has been missed at that point in preparing the working diagram, particularly as it is less easy to check connections on a working diagram than on a theoretical circuit diagram.

The theoretical circuit diagram, however, remains the check reference for the working plan — and for checking the circuit when built. It may also be the only guide available for establishing the correct way to connect a diode or a polarized capacitor (electrolytic capacitor). Following the direction of current flow (and thus the polarity at any particular point), should be fairly straightforward, re-

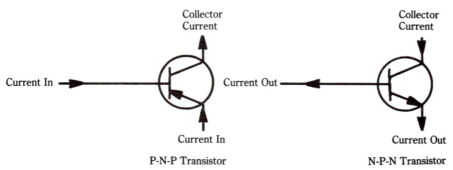

Fig. 18-8. Direction of current flow through PNP and NPN transistors.

membering that with a + top line, the direction of current flow is downwards (from top line to bottom line), through various components on such paths. If the top line is —, the flow direction is obviously reversed. It is also easy to check the direction of current flow through transistors by the arrow on the emitter in the transistor symbol. Direction of current flow *out* of the transistor via the collector follows in the same direction. Direction of current flow *into* the base of the transistor is opposite to that of the emitter arrow direction. Figure 18-8 should make this clear.

These rules for reading the current flow through transistors should also make it fairly simple to determine the current flow with horizontally connected components on the circuit diagram, and thus establish the correct polarity for electrolytic capacitors appearing in these lines.

19
Circuit Construction

One of the big problems facing most beginners is how to construct a working circuit; i.e., turn a theoretical circuit diagram into a connected-up assembly of components (with all the connections correct, of course!).

The following diagrams show six very simple and straightforward methods of tackling elementary circuit construction — all capable of giving good results with the minimum of trouble, and especially recommended for absolute beginners at practical electronics.

PINBOARD CONSTRUCTION

Draw out the component layout for the circuit on a piece of thin ply (or even hard balsa sheet), using a ballpoint pen (*not* a lead pencil). Draw in all connections and mark points where common connections occur with a blob (just as on circuit diagrams).

Cut out the panel to a suitable size. Drive copper tacks into each blob and simply solder the components in position. Complete additional connections with plain wire, see Fig. 19-1.

SKELETON ASSEMBLY

Start again with a component drawing, this time on paper. Lay components in place, bending the leads of resistors and capacitors to complete connections. Other connections can be complete with two lengths of 16-gauge copper wire for

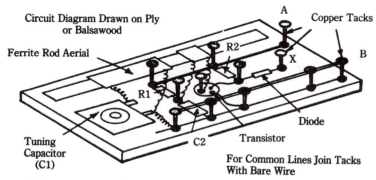

Fig. 19-1. Pinboard construction starts by drawing a working plan of the circuit on a panel of ply or balsa. Then drive in copper tacks at each connection point. Solder component leads to tacks, and complete circuit as necessary with any additional wiring.

"top" and "bottom" control lines. Solder all the connecting points, adding transistors last (Fig. 19-2). Properly done, such a skeleton assembly can be quite rigid.

BONDED MOUNTING

This is very similar to skeleton assembly except that individual resistors and capacitors are stuck down to a rigid base panel cut from plastic sheet. Use five-minute epoxy for gluing the components in place (Fig. 19-3). This produces a very strong bond in a few minutes. With the main components rigidly mounted, you can then bend leads to produce the necessary connections and connection points for other components (e.g., transistors).

BUS-BAR ASSEMBLY

This is a neat and more professional way to tackle circuit construction. The top and bottom common lines of the circuit are laid down first by mounting two lengths of 16-gauge tinned copper wire in a sheet of plastic as shown. This

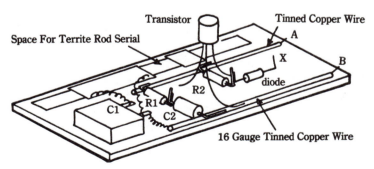

Fig. 19-2. The same circuit as Fig. 19-1 tackled by just connecting components together via their open leads, and using bare wire for top and bottom lines.

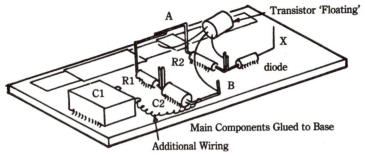

Fig. 19-3. Bonded mounting is similar to Fig. 19-2 but all components (except transistors) are glued down to a base panel. Turn up ends of leads to form connecting points.

permits most of the resistors and capacitors to be mounted with one lead soldered in place. Complete the rest of the connections as for skeleton assembly (Fig. 19-4).

TAGBOARD ASSEMBLY

More durable and neater than the previous methods, this involves mounting strips of solder tags (called tag strips) at each of the main connecting points of the circuit layout. These tags can be riveted or bolted through the panel. Individual components are then mounted between tags. Any additional connections are formed by short lengths of wire between tags (Fig. 19-5). More time is needed to construct a proper tagboard than with the previous methods, but complete tagboard stops are also available with up to 36 individual tags mounted in two parallel rows.

PEGBOARD CONSTRUCTION

You can buy special terminal pillars to press into the holes in ordinary pegboard and so set up connecting points for mounting components (Fig. 19-6).

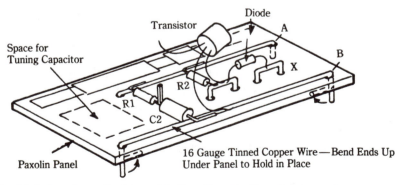

Fig. 19-4. Lay down the top and bottom lines in tinned copper wire, permanently mounted on the panel. Shorter lengths of bare wire can be used for other common connecting points. Complete by soldering component leads in place.

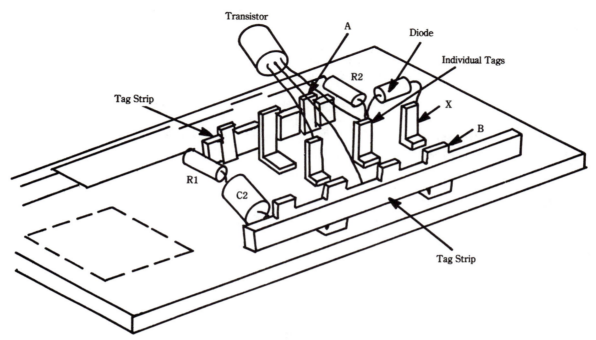

Fig. 19-5. *All the connecting points are formed by tag strips or individual tags mounted on the panel. Solder components to appropriate tags, and complete with additional wiring as necessary.*

These terminals have screw connecting points, so you can avoid soldering components in place. The main disadvantage is that a fairly large panel size is needed, even for a simple circuit, with components spread out. But it is an easy method of building experimental circuits.

There are various proprietary systems based on variations of the pegboard method. *Veroboards* are panels with rows of copper strips, each strip drilled with a number of holes either 1 mm (0.04 in.) or 1.3 mm (0.052 in.) diameter. Matching pins (Veropins) can be inserted in appropriate holes to form terminal pillars, and the copper strips cut as necessary to separate connecting points. Special tools are used for inserting the Veropins and for cutting the copper strips. *Verostrip* is a similar type of board except that the board is narrower (1½ in. wide) and the copper strips run across the board with a break down the center. Components can be mounted across or along the strips.

Numerous solderless breadboards have also been developed where component leads are simply pushed into the boards where they are held by spring contacts. Contact points are arranged in parallel rows, with either a prearranged pattern of interconnection, or with basic busbar connections on top and bottom rows and others in common groups. Interconnection between groups can be made by wires pushed into spare points in each separate group.

The advantage of such a system is that, apart from avoiding soldering, circuits can easily be modified simply by pulling out a component and plugging into a different position.

For permanent circuits, if you're a beginner, you will probably find pegboard assembly the best proposition after you have gained some experience in circuit construction—and confidence in being able to draw out component layouts accurately.

The ultimate for all forms of compact circuit construction is, however, the printed circuit. Here components are mounted directly through holes in a plastic (or glass fiber) panel on which the circuit wiring has been reproduced by etching. This is a separate technique on its own, but easy enough to learn (see Chapter 20).

GENERAL RULES

Connections should *always* be soldered for best results. This applies even on pegboards fitted with screw-type terminal pillars. The one exception to the rule

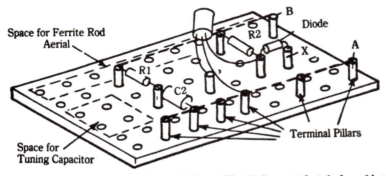

Fig. 19-6. Pegboard assembly is similar to Fig. 19-5 except that the board is predrilled to accept terminal posts. Locate these posts at suitable points to act as common connecting points. Connect components to posts, then complete the additional wiring as necessary. Note: all these constructional drawings show the same circuit—a simple single-transistor radio receiver with preamplifier. Components required are:

> *Ferrite rod aerial with coupling coil*
> *C1 = 0-500 pF tuning capacitor*
> *C2 = 0.01 microfarad*
> *R1 = 1 Megohm*
> *R2 = 2.2 k*
> *Diode = any germanium crystal diode*
> *Transistor = any rf transistor*

The circuit works off a 9-volt battery connected to A and B (polarity depends on whether the transistor used is a PNP or NPN type). For listening, connect high impedance head-phones to points X and B.

In case the aerial coil connections are not clear:

- *The ends of the main coil connect to the two tags on the tuning capacitor (C1)*
- *One end of the coupling coil connects to the common connecting point of R1 and C2*
- *The other end of the coupling coil connects to the base lead (b) of the transistor*

is solderless breadboards where connections are made by spring clips. In any case, never rely on joints which are formed simply by twisting wires together.

Use a small electric soldering iron for making all soldered joints, and resin-cored solder (electrical grade). Never use an acid type flux on soldered joints in electrical circuits.

Transistors can be damaged by excessive heat. When soldering in place to a circuit, leave the leads quite long (at least 1 inch). Grip each lead with flat nose pliers behind the joint when soldering. The jaws of the pliers then act as a heatsink, preventing overheating of the transistor. Once you are proficient at soldering, however, this precaution should not be necessary, especially in the case of silicon transistors.

The most common reason why a particular circuit does not work is because one or more connections have been wrongly made. This is far more likely to be the cause of the trouble than a faulty component. Always check over all connections after you have made them, using the theoretical circuit diagram as the basic reference. Also, with transistor circuits, *be sure* to connect the battery the right way (as shown on the circuit diagram).

20
Printed Circuits

The stock material for making printed circuit boards (PCBs) is copper-clad phenolic resin laminate (SRBP) or glass-fiber laminate. For general use, these boards are single-sided (clad on one side only) and nominally 1.5 mm thick (about $\frac{1}{16}$ in.). The procedure for making a PCB involves:

1. Cutting the board to the required size and cleaning the copper surface.
2. Making a drawing of the conductors required for the circuit on the copper in a *resist* ink.
3. Etching away uncovered copper areas in a chemical bath.
4. Removing the resist ink to expose the copper conducting areas or pads.
5. Drilling the copper pads ready to take the component leads.
6. Degreasing and cleaning the boards as necessary to ensure that the pads take solder readily.

PLANNING THE CIRCUIT DRAWING

Familiarity with the physical size of components to be accommodated on the board is essential, so that holes for leads, etc, can be correctly positioned. There are two ways in which resistors and capacitors can be mounted: horizontally or vertically (Fig. 20-1). Horizontal mounting is usual for resistors as this reduces lead length to a minimum. Holes are then spaced a sufficient distance apart to allow for easy 90-degree finger-bends on the leads. The same consideration applied to tubular capacitors, mounted horizontally.

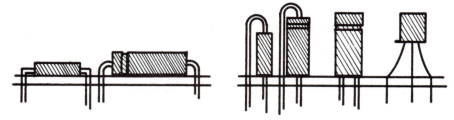

Fig. 20-1. Horizontal mounting of components on a PC board takes up more space, but is usually more convenient than vertical mounting (except for transistors).

The physical size of capacitors, however, may be much larger than resistors, when vertical mounting may be preferred to save space. Mounting holes then only need to be a little more than half the diameter of the capacitor, matching the position of the top lead taken down the side of the capacitor. Some capacitors have both leads emerging from the same end, especially for vertical mounting on a PCB. Spacing between holes, however, should not be less than twice the thickness of the board (i.e., ⅛ in.).

Transistors need reasonably wide spacing for their leads. Exceptions are transistor types with leads intended to plug directly into a PCB, and certain power transistors needing special mounts. In these cases, hole positioning follows the transistor lead geometry. Integrated circuits normally plug directly into matching IC sockets, the latter being mounted on the board in holes drilled to match the pin positions.

Layout starts with a tentative design of component positions, sketching in the connections required, (i.e., the areas of copper which will eventually form the conducting pads). No connections on a PCB can cross, and a certain amount of trial-and-error sketching is usually needed to achieve this requirement, altering component positions as necessary. If it seems impossible to achieve a complete circuit without crossing connections, then such points can be terminated on the PC drawing on each side of the crossing point, and subsequently completed during assembly of the circuit by bridging with a short length of insulated wire, just as a component normally acts as a bridge between adjacent conductors (Fig. 20-2).

Insulated
Wire

Fig. 20-2. If it is (or seems) impossible to avoid a crossing connection on a PC board, stop the crossing lines short (left) and complete the connection with a bridge of insulated wire soldered in place.

FINAL DRAWING

Having arrived at a suitable layout, with connecting points for component leads indicated by blobs (·), a tracing can then be made of this PCB plan. Certain general rules apply in preparing the final drawing:

1. Conductors should not be less than 1/16 inch wide.
2. Conductors should be spaced at least 1/32 inch apart.
3. There should be at least 1/32 inch between a conductor and the edge of a panel.
4. Bends of junctions in conductors should be radiused or filleted, not sharp-edged.
5. Allow sufficient area of copper around a connecting point so that the copper width at this point is at least twice that of the hole size subsequently to be drilled through it, and preferably more. (Typical hole sizes for miniature resistors, capacitors and transistors are 1/32 inch).

These points are illustrated in Fig. 20-3.

It is not necessary to draw all conductors neatly and uniform in thickness. Relatively large solid areas can be left to accommodate a number of common connecting points, simplifying the amount of drawing necessary (Fig. 21-4). Large solid areas should, however, be avoided in any part of a circuit carrying high current as this could cause excessive heating of the copper, possibly making it delaminate as it expands. Thus, on a PCB for a mains-operated circuit, for example, the maximum area of any particular copper pad should not be more than about 1 square inch.

The final drawing is transferred in reverse on to the copper (hence the use of tracing paper). This is because the circuit, as originally planned, shows the *component* side of the board, which is the plain side. Thus the true pattern for the

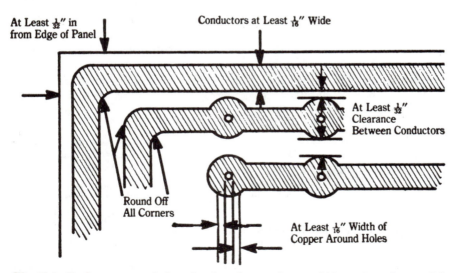

Fig. 20-3. Basic recommendations for planning conductor widths and spacings on PC boards.

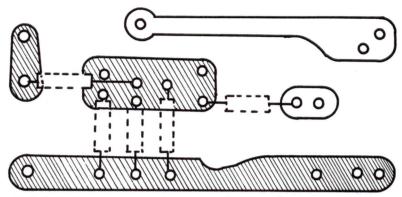

Fig. 20-4. Quite large areas of copper can be left on low voltage battery powered circuits. There is no need for consistent widths (or shapes) of conductors.

copper side is reversed, mirror-image fashion. But before transferring the drawing to the board, the copper surface must be cleaned. This is done by washing with detergent and then drying.

A test for cleanliness is to hold the board copper-side up under a tap and let water run on to it. If the water flows freely over the whole area, it is free from grease. If dry patches appear on the copper, these areas are still greasy and require further cleaning.

After tracing the (reversed image) pattern on to the copper, this pattern is then painted in with resist ink or a *resist marker pen* (much easier to use than a brush and ink). Make sure that all the pad areas are properly filled, but avoid applying too much ink as this could overrun the required outlines. Finally, allow to dry, which should take about 10 to 15 minutes.

ETCHING

The board is then transferred to an *etching bath*. This can consist of a solution of ferric chloride, or proprietary printed circuit etching fluid poured into a shallow plastic tray. The board is placed in the bath copper side up and left until all traces of copper have disappeared from the surface. Time taken for this will vary with the temperature of the solution and its strength. The process can be speeded up by rocking the bath gently or stirring with a soft brush.

After etching is completed the board is removed, washed under running water to remove any traces of chemical, and dried with a soft cloth. The etching solution can be kept for re-use, if required.

To remove the resist ink, a further liquid known as etch-resist remover should be used. This can be brushed on to the board and then rubbed with a soft cloth, or applied to the cloth first and then rubbed over the board. It should only take a minute or so to remove all the ink, leaving the copper patterns fully uncovered and clean. Wash and dry the board again at this stage to remove any residual traces of etch-resist remover.

Drilling comes next. The following rules are very important:

- Always drill with the copper side uppermost; i.e., drill through the copper into the board.
- Always use a sharp drill bit (preferably a new one).
- Always use a backing of hard material under the board to prevent the point of the drill from tearing a lump out of the back of the board when the point breaks through.
- Spot the point to be drilled with a small center punch to prevent the drill running off its correct position when starting to drill.

Use of an electric drill in a vertical drill stand is best for drilling PCBs. However, because of the small size of drill used, breakage rate of drills can be high if the work is pushed too hard.

The original tracing comes in handy again for marking the component positions on the plain side of the board, as a guide for component assembly (Fig. 20-5). Components are always assembled on the plain side, with their leads pushed through their mounting holes until the component is lying flush with the board (Fig. 20-1). The exception is transistors, which should be mounted with their leads left fairly long (and preferably with each lead insulated with a length of sleeving to prevent accidental shorting if the transistor is displaced).

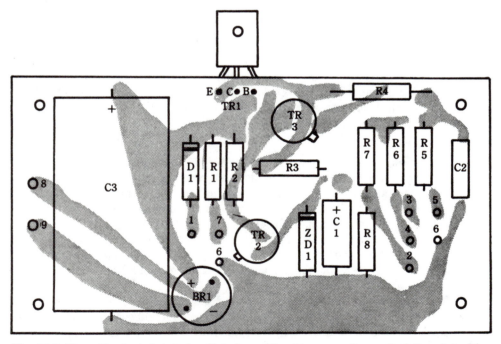

Fig. 20-5. Example of a printed circuit design with copper area shown shaded and position of components indicated.

144

MOUNTING AND SOLDERING

Before mounting components in position for soldering, the copper side should be cleaned again. It will probably have picked up grease marks through handling. An ordinary domestic powder cleaner is best for this, used wet or dry, and rubbed on with a soft cloth. The running water test can again be used as a check for cleanliness, but if the board is wetted, dry with a cloth.

Components are normally soldered in place, one at a time, with their full lead length protruding. Excess length of wire is then cut off as close as possible to the solder.

Provided soldered joints are completed rapidly, in not more than about 3 seconds, heat-damage to either the board or a component is unlikely. If the iron has to be held in contact with the lead for longer than this, then something is wrong with the soldering technique and heat damage could result, either to the component or by the lifting of the copper pad on the PCB. The most likely causes of overheating are using an iron which is not hot enough or too small for the job; attempting to rework a soldered joint which has not taken properly; and trying to remove a lead which has been soldered into the wrong hole.

SIMPLIFIED PRINTED CIRCUIT CONSTRUCTION

As a supplement to drawing — and for making neater straight lines — there rub-off transfer sheets of lines, bends, blobs for connecting points, etc. are available, which can be used to build up the required pattern on the copper, supplemented with ink drawing where necessary. These transfer symbols are resistant to etching fluid, so serve the same function as drawn or painted lines.

It is also possible to buy self-adhesive copper foil precut in the form of lines, bends, etc, similar to transfer strips, but which can be pressed down on to a plain panel to complete a printed circuit directly, without the need for any etching treatment. Further shapes can be cut from self-adhesive copper foil blanks. With PC boards made up in this fashion continuous (conductor) sections can be made up from overlapping pieces, provided positive connection is made by solder applied over the joint line.

21
Radio

Radio broadcasts consist of a radio frequency (rf) signal generated at a specific frequency allocated to a particular station, on which is superimposed an *audio frequency (af)* signal.

Only rf works for *transmission*. The af part, which is the actual sound content of the signal is, almost literally, carried on the back of the rf signal, the two together forming what is called a *modulated* signal.

This combined signal can be produced in two different ways — amplitude, or up-and-down modulation, known as AM; and frequency modulation (actually a very small variation in rf signal frequency about its station frequency), known as FM.

AM is the simpler technique and is widely used for long wave, medium wave and short wave broadcasts. Broadcasting has always been referred to in terms of wavelengths instead of signal frequency, until comparatively recently. The relationship between wavelength and frequency is:

$$\text{wavelengths (meters)} = \frac{300,000,000}{\text{frequency, Hz}}$$

$$\text{frequency, Hz} = \frac{300,000,000}{\text{wavelength, meters}}$$

(The figure 300,000 is the speed of light in meters per second, which is the speed at which radio frequency waves travel.)

In the case of FM, very high transmitting frequencies are used—and it is generally referred to as VHF (very high frequency). Actual *wavelengths* are very short, and so it is much more convenient to speak of frequency, the usual range for FM broadcasts being 90–100 million Hertz (90–100 MHz). A simple calculation shows that this means a wavelength of about 3.2 to 2.9 meters, or about 3 meters.

Regardless of whether the broadcast is AM or FM, any radio frequency signal has the same basic requirement for receiving it. The presence of this signal has to be "found" and then sorted out from signals from other broadcast stations. The "finding" device is the antenna, and the "sorting out" device is the *tuned circuit*. Together, they form the front end of a radio receiver as shown in Fig. 21-1 (the extreme left-hand part of a circuit diagram—see also Chapter 18).

A *tuned circuit* consists, basically, of a coil and variable capacitor, which can be adjusted to show resonance or maximum response to a particular signal frequency applied to it. A full explanation of this behavior is given in Chapter 7. All the broadcast signals reaching the tuned circuit are very, very weak. Only that signal to which it is *tuned* is magnified by resonance, so that it stands out at a very much higher level of signal strength.

An actual wire antenna connected to the tuned circuit may or may not be necessary. In the case of AM reception, the coil winding also acts as an efficient wire antenna, if wound on a ferrite rod. This dispenses with the need for an external antenna. The only disadvantage is that the tuned circuit is *directional,* minimum signal strength being received when the ferrite rod is pointing towards the transmitter sending the signal, and maximum signal strength when the ferrite rod is at right angles to this direction. This effect is most noticeable on small radio receivers which have only moderate amplification. To receive certain

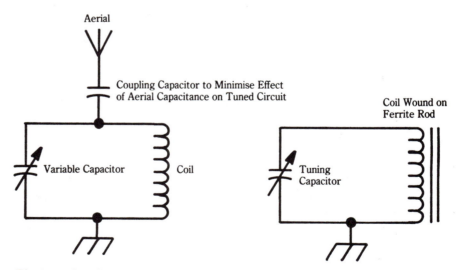

Fig. 21-1. A variable capacitor and coil form the usual tuned circuit. Strictly speaking this tunes the antenna, if an external aerial wire is used. Most AM receivers use a ferrite rod antenna which does not require an external antenna.

stations at good listening level, even with maximum adjustment of volume, it may be necessary to adjust the position of the set. Larger receivers normally have enough amplification to compensate for this, but the effect can still be quite noticeable. Also, it is always best to operate a receiver below maximum amplification because this minimizes distortion of the signal.

The FM receiver *does* need an external antenna because a wound coil or a ferrite rod antenna just does not work at this rf. For satisfactory results, this external antenna also needs to be a special type, known as a dipole, which itself is tuned by making its length one half of the *signal wavelength.* The latter may vary from 11.5 feet to 9.5 feet in the 90 – 100 MHz FM band, so a mean wavelength figure of about 10 feet is adopted, giving a realistic dipole length of 5 feet.

The three practical FM antenna forms are a vertical telescopic aerial extending to 30 inches; a horizontal wire (or rod antenna) with 30 inch legs; or a folded dipole, as shown in Fig. 21-2.

DETECTION

The tuned circuit is much simpler than the foregoing descriptions may appear to imply. It is really a matter of getting the component values right, and working with high efficiency (see also Chapter 6 and Q-factor). Design of the tuned circuit is a little more complicated when a radio is intended to receive more than one waveband. Even an AM receiver needs separate antenna coils (or at least separated wings on a single ferrite rod) to cover long wave, medium wave, and shortwave. So the tuned circuit design for an AM receiver could involve three or more tuned circuits selectable by a switch.

In the case of an FM receiver (or the tuning circuit for the FM section of a multi-band receiver), there is really no practical form of wound antenna coil which can be used (a theoretical coil of this type would probably require only a part of a single turn). So the starting point is a dipole antenna. This itself is a tuned circuit (i.e., designed to be resonant with the mean frequency to be

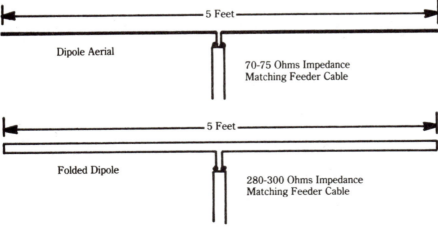

Fig. 21-2. FM antennas need connecting to the set via a correctly matched feeder cable.

covered in the FM band), but its amplification of signal is not nearly as good as that of the coil-and-capacitor tuned circuit of an AM receiver.

To compensate for this, the FM receiver normally uses an amplifier stage immediately following the aerial, known as a preamplifier or rf amplifier (because it is an amplifier of signals at radio frequency). This amplified signal is fed to the next stage of the receiver via a tuned output. A typical circuit of this type is shown in Fig. 21-3.

The *detector* stage following the tuned circuit can be extremely simple. In the case of AM, it only needs to be a diode connected to a potentiometer as its load. This potentiometer also acts as the volume control—Fig. 21-4.

The signal passed on from the tuned circuit to the detector is a strengthened version of the original modulated broadcast signal. In other words, it contains both af and rf. The rf part has now done its job in getting the signal into the tuned circuit. Now it needs to be removed, which can be done by rectifying the signal. A diode does this job by chopping off one half of the rf signal so that the output from the diode consists of half-cycles of rf. These half cycles have the af content of the signal still imposed, so the next requirement is to filter out the rf part to turn the output into an undulating dc signal. These undulations follow exactly the same variations as the af signal originally imposed on the transmitter rf signal at the transmitting station by a microphone, or recording.

As explained in Chapter 6, a resistor and capacitor can act as a filter for any specific frequency required. Thus the diode detector is associated with a matching load (resistance) and associated capacitor forming the required filter circuit;

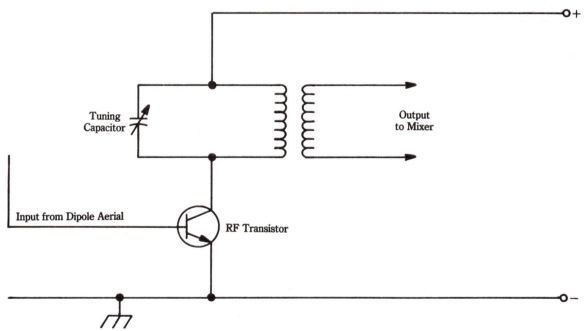

Fig. 21-3. Basic rf amplifier (or preamplifier) circuit as used in many FM receivers.

e.g., see Fig. 21-4 — so that only varying dc is passed at output from the detector stage. It is usually coupled to the next stage by a capacitor, which has the further effect of balancing the varying dc signal about its zero line (i.e., giving it positive and negative values, rather than "all positive values").

In practice, the output load (R in Fig. 21-4) is usually a variable resistor, which component then also acts as a volume control. The fact that this is followed by a coupling capacitor also avoids any flow of dc through the moving contact (wiper) of this control and reduces any tendency to reproduce noise by movement of this control.

The aim in selecting the detector circuit components is that the signal passed by the diode is exactly the same as the original signal generated by the studio microphone (with certain losses and possible distortions!). Fed to a microphone working in reverse (i.e., headphones or a loudspeaker) they would be heard as the original speech or music. But the signals at this stage are still too weak to have enough power to drive headphones or a loudspeaker, so the next step is to amplify the af signal passed by the detector.

FM DETECTOR

In the case of an FM receiver, the detector is a little more complicated. It has to detect how the *frequency* of the signal is varying, not its amplitude, so it has to extract the original frequency as well as apply rectification. FM receivers invariably work on the superhet principle, so the frequency to be extracted is the intermediate frequency of if. A basic detector circuit employs a three-winding transformer with primary and secondary tuned to the intermediate frequency (by capacitors C1 and C2 in Fig. 21-5). The third winding injects a voltage into the secondary circuit, each leg of which carries a diode, D1 and D2, associated with a capacitor C3 and C4.

The working of this circuit is to detect variations in signal frequency in terms of an af output, so that the final output is exactly the same, in terms of signal content, as that from an AM detector. Thus it can be dealt with in the same way.

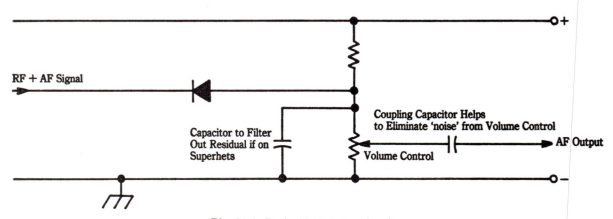

Fig. 21-4. Basic AM detector circuit.

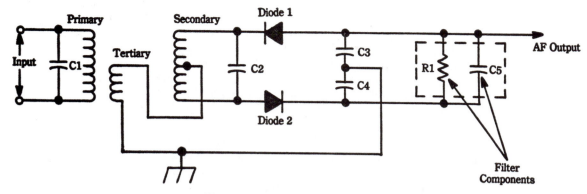

Fig. 21-5. Basic FM detector circuit.

The additional components R1 and C5 shown on the diagram are to suppress unwanted signals which may be present after detection.

AMPLIFIER STAGES

A single transistor can provide amplification of signal strength up to 100 times or more (see Chapter 9 for typical amplifier circuits). The main requirement of the amplifier following the detector is that the transistor be specifically suitable for amplifying af (when it can act as a further block to any residual rf remaining in the input signal to the amplifier). Ideally, there should be no rf signal present at the input to the amplifier stage (it should have been filtered out in the detector stage), since any rf voltage presented to the amplifier stage could cause overloading.

Theoretically, at least, any amount of amplification can be produced by adding additional transistor-amplifier stages (Fig. 21-6). This does, however, greatly increase the chances of distorting the signal, so there are practical limits to the number of stages which are acceptable in simple circuits. Much better results can be produced by more sophisticated circuits, particularly the superhet (see below), where first some intermediate signal is amplified *before* detection; and subsequently amplified again *after* detection.

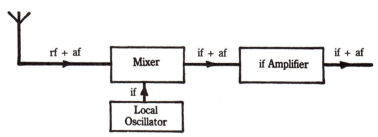

Fig. 21-6. Adding amplifier stages is not necessarily a good thing for amplifying an af signal as each stage can amplify distortion produced in the previous stage.

151

OUTPUT STAGE

The af amplifier output (or last af amplifier stage output if more than one stage is used) can develop enough power to drive a loudspeaker, as in Fig. 21-6, although there may be some problem in matching the (amplifier) output to the (loudspeaker) input, particularly using low to medium power transistors which require a high impedance load to match. Most loudspeakers have a load imped-ance of only 4 – 16 ohms. A basic solution here is to use an output transformer to match the different load characteristics, as in Fig. 21-7.

This relatively simple solution does, however, have one particular limitation (for the more technically minded, it is called a Class A output). It is relatively inefficient and so draws a high current in providing a suitable listening level from the loudspeaker. It is satisfactory for use in car radios, but represents too heavy a current drain for most other battery-powered receivers.

These normally use a Class B output circuit where the last amplifier transistor drives a pair of transistors which effectively work in a push-pull circuit operating the loudspeaker. The output power obtained is considerably more than double the power available from a single transistor; also, and output transformer is not necessary. Most modern af amplifiers for radios end up in a push-pull output stage of this type, like the circuit shown in Fig. 21-8.

The limitations of simple radio receivers are mainly connected with the limita-tion of a detector. A detector is most effective working with an rf input voltage of

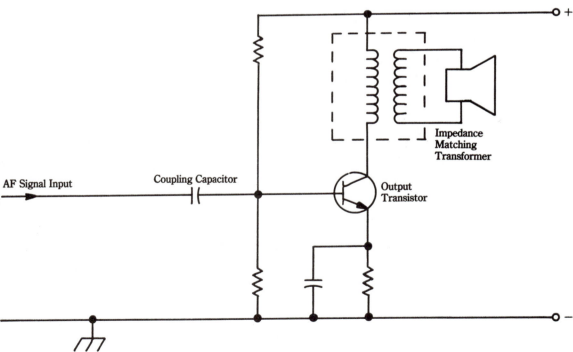

Fig. 21-7. Basic class A output circuit.

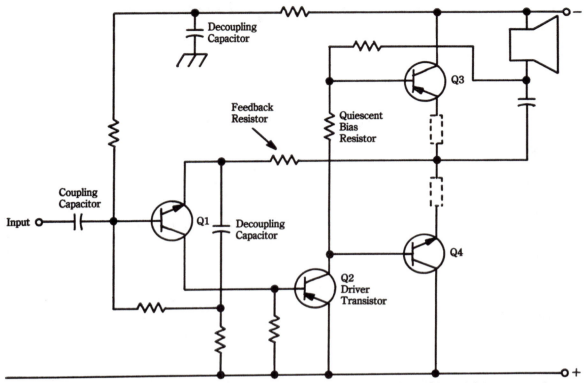

Fig. 21-8. Basic class B output circuit. Q1 acts as a preamplifier. Q2 is the driver. Q3 and Q4 are a complementary pair of transistors, working alternately in "push-pull." The two resistors shown by dashed lines may be added to improve the stability of the circuit. These only need to be of very low value (e.g., 1 ohm).

1 volt or more. Signals derived directly from an antenna circuit are seldom more than a few millivolts in strength, and the weaker the signal the less effectively they will be detected in any case. In other words, the range of stations that can be picked up is limited, and no amount of amplification *after* detection can make up for this limitation.

This limitation, or lack of *sensitivity,* can be overcome by amplifying the incoming signal before detection, so that the detector is always working with good signal strength. This can be done by rf amplification of the antenna signal by introducing an amplifier stage right at the beginning of the circuit as in the FM receiver (Fig. 21-3); or by the superhet working. The latter also improves the *selectivity* of a receiver, or its ability to tune in sharply to wanted signals and reject nearby station signals.

THE SUPERHET

Having arrived at a standardized output stage, it is equally true to say that nearly all modern radio receivers are of the *superhet* type, which is considerably more complicated than the circuit traced through above. The whole front end works on an entirely different principle.

Starting point is the tuned circuit (ferrite rod antenna) in the case of an AM receiver; or a dipole antenna feeding an rf amplifier in the case of an FM receiver (the latter amplifying the modulated radio signal in conjunction with a tuned resonant circuit). In both cases the boosted tuned signal is fed to an *oscillator-mixer*.

This is a two-function circuit, although its duty is usually performed by a single transistor associated with a tuned oscillator circuit. This tuned circuit is mechanically coupled to the antenna tuning in the form of a ganged capacitor (i.e., two separate variable capacitors coupled, or ganged to move together when the tuning control is adjusted), so that it tracks the aerial circuit tuning while remaining separated from it *by a constant frequency*. This difference is known as the *intermediate frequency* or i-f, and is usually 455 kHz above the aerial frequency (it can have other values in certain sets, and can also be below rather than above the antenna frequency).

The oscillator part of the oscillator-mixer is concerned with generating this fixed intermediate frequency, tracking exactly above (or below) the signal frequency to which the aerial circuit is tuned. The two signals are combined in the mixer part of the oscillator-mixer, which also has a *fixed* tuned circuit (actually the primary side of a transformer associated with a capacitor) which responds only to the intermediate frequency — Fig. 21-9. This i-f signal also now has the same af modulation as the original signal. In other words, it is a duplicate of the wanted af signal, but at this stage superimposed on a fixed intermediate frequency.

There are a number of technical advantages to this seemingly unnecessary complication of incoming signal treatment. First, the process of superheterodyning gives much better *selectivity* or rejection of unwanted signals. Then, the signal output from the mixer is at a constant frequency, making it easy to amplify with the further possibility of eliminating any remaining unwanted frequencies since an i-f amplifier has fixed — and virtually exact — tuning.

In practice, i-f amplification is usually carried out in two stages (AM receivers) or three stages (FM receivers). The detector then follows after the i-f amplifier stages — Fig. 21-10. Each i-f amplifier stage consists of a tuned transformer, adjustment of tuning being done by an iron dust core in the transformer coil former. Once correctly adjusted, the cores are sealed in this position.

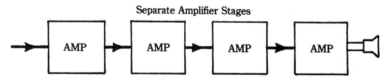
Separate Amplifier Stages

Fig. 21-9. Front end of a superhet receiver, showing how the incoming rf plus af signal is transformed into an af signal now imposed on a fixed intermediate frequency (i-f). This makes amplification without distortion more simple to achieve.

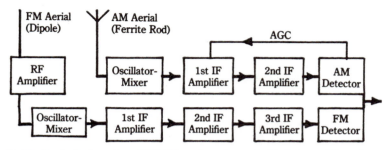

Fig. 21-10. Basic design of an AM/FM receiver shown in block form. The only common circuit is an af amplifier (usually a class B output) following the detectors.

The remainder of the radio circuit follows as before—rf amplifier stage(s) following the detector, terminating in (usually) a push-pull output stage. But there is just one further refinement which can be added. By feeding a proportion of the signal passed by the detector back to the first i-f amplifier stage, automatic volume control (normally called automatic gain control or *agc*) can be achieved. If the signal strength passed by the detector starts to rise to a point where it could become distorted, then feedback via the agc line automatically reduces the amount of signal entering at this point, so maintaining the detector working under optimum conditions.

Agc applies only to the control of amplification of signal in the i-f amplifier stages. The output or gain of the final i-f amplifier stage(s) is governed by a separate volume control (potentiometer), typically located before the first af amplifier stage. This potentiometer, incidentally, usually has a capacitor connected in parallel with it to filter out any residual i-f which may have got past the detector.

22
Television

Television makes special use of a *cathode ray tube,* which in turn has certain characteristics in common with a vacuum tube (see Chapter 12). It has a heater, a cathode which emits electrons, an anode to which electrons are attracted, and a control grid. Unlike a tube, however, the electrons are directed at the enlarged end of the tube *or screen* which is coated with a *phosphor* material.

It is, in fact, a special type of cathode ray tube. The narrow end of the tube acts as an electron gun, shooting electrons past the anode section. Electrons impinging on the screen generate more electrons which are attracted back to the anode, equivalent in effect to each electron reaching the screen being bounced back to the anode. Thus no electrons, and hence no charge, actually collect on the screen. Meantime, however, each electron reaching the screen makes the phosphor glow, which persists for a short period after the electron has been bounced back.

The brightness of the glow produced is dependent on the type of phosphor (which also governs the color of the glow), and the strength of bombardment of electrons. The latter is controlled by the bias voltage applied to the grid. In other words, grid bias adjustment is the brightness control on a TV tube (Fig. 22-1). The actual brightness is also enhanced by an extremely thin layer of aluminum deposited over the phosphor to act rather like an outward-facing mirror, but transparent from the other side as far as electrons are concerned.

To produce a picture from electron bombardment, two other controls are necessary. The first is a means of deflecting the electron beam so that a single spot can trace out a particular path covering all the variations in picture density

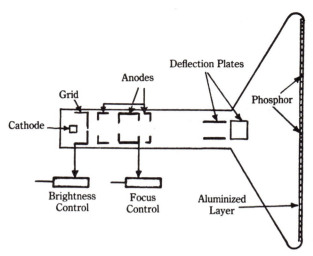

Fig. 22-1. The TV tube and its basic controls, shown in simplified form.

over the whole screen area. The second is a means of focusing the electron beam into a tiny spot so that the traced picture is sharp, not fuzzy.

Deflection is achieved by directing the stream of electrons through two sets of parallel coils set at right angles to each other like the X and Y deflection plates in a simple cathode ray tube (Chapter 12). Signal voltages applied to the X-coils deflect the beam sideways; signal voltages applied to the Y-coils deflect the beam vertically. Combined X and Y signals thus direct the beam toward any spot on the screen, depending on the resultant effect of the two signals.

Focusing, meantime, is achieved by using supplementary cylindrical anodes arranged to work as an electronic lens, with the focusing effect adjustable by varying the voltage applied to one (or more) of these anodes. These anodes come before the deflection plates; i.e., in the parallel or gun section of the tube rather than in the divergent section.

Electronic circuits can respond very rapidly — which is how television can be made to work at all! To paint a picture on the screen a spot of light (produced by a focused electron beam) has to traverse the whole picture area, zig-zag fashion, at least 30 times per second if the picture is to appear reasonably free of flicker. It does this in a number of parallel lines, usually running from left to right, with rapid flyback between lines, Fig. 22-2. The greater the number of lines the clearer the picture will be, i.e., the better the *definition*. The standard commonly adopted in the United States is 525 lines (per picture). The actual frequency at which lines appear, called the *line frequency,* is $30 \times 525 = 15750$ per second. This line pattern is known as a *raster.* The lines making up the raster can actually be seen if you examine the television screen close up, or turn up the brightness control when no picture is being transmitted. Only the parallel lines can be seen in the raster. During flyback, the cathode ray tube is cut off and no lines appear on the screen.

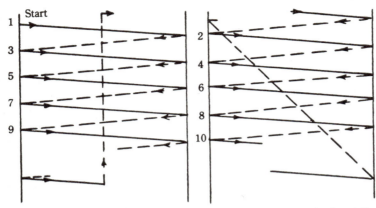

Fig. 22-2. Illustrating the formation of a raster. First the odd numbered lines are scanned from left to right (solid lines) with flyback between each line (dashed lines). Downward movement is controlled by the time base. After scanning half the picture lines, the time base flies back to the top. All the even number lines are then scanned, with flyback between each line (right hand diagram). At the end of the last line the time base flies back to the left to start the sequence all over again. These two diagrams superimposed represent a complete raster.

In practice the picture is scanned 60 times per second, not 30. This is fast enough to eliminate any trace of flicker, but using an optical trick, the actual *picture frequency* is still only 30 per second. Scanning takes place in two stages —first the odd lines only, then the even lines. Each scan therefore builds up only half the picture, the two halves following each other to present the complete picture.

Movement of the lines downwards is accomplished by the *time base* circuit starting with the first (odd) line and restarting a line at the left *two* positions down each time. This continues until the scanning has reached $525 \div 2 = 262\frac{1}{2}$ lines. The spot then flies back to the top again, starting half way along the first even line and repeats the process to scan the $262\frac{1}{2}$ even lines which make up the second half of the picture. This process is known as *interlacing.* Actually a few lines get left out in this changeover process, but this does not show up on the picture.

Picture transmission and picture reception operate in reverse mode. The television camera scans the scene to be transmitted in 525 lines at a picture frequency of 30 per second, and turns the light spot response into electrical signals. The number of lines has been quoted as governing picture definition, but this is not the whole story. A scan of 525 lines gives good picture definition from top to bottom, e.g., the picture is built up top-to-bottom from 525 strips. There is also the question of how many individual picture elements are covered by each strip. The answer is about 600 as an absolute minimum for good picture definition side-to-side, or the equivalent of 600 phosphor dots making up each line. The total number of individual dots or picture elements in each whole picture trace is thus 315,000. Since the picture frequency is 30 times per second, this calls for a transmitted signal frequency of 2.5 MHz.

These intelligence signals are broadcast like any other radio transmission—superimposed on a *carrier wave* to produce a modulated signal which can be picked up by a receiver and decoded on a similar principle to ordinary radio reception, except that the decoder now has to handle radio frequencies of 2.5 MHz and not af signals, so the TV receiver decoder is considerably more complicated than a radio receiver detector.

There is also another important difference. Carrier wave frequencies have to be much higher than modulation frequencies for satisfactory results. Hence the frequency of television picture signals is in the VHF range. It is invariably an AM broadcast with sidebands, operating within a channel width of 8 MHz. Either AM or FM can be used for the accompanying sound signal (FM is standard).

The fairly wide channel width or frequency spread occupied by a television transmission does not make it susceptible to receiving spurious signals upsetting the picture (but not the sound, which is operating in a narrow band like any ordinary FM receiver). It also limits the number of television stations that can be accommodated in the VHF band without interfering with each other.

This particular consideration also makes the design of a color television system even more complicated than it need be using first-principle electronics. For example, it would mean expanding the bandwidth to three times its black-and-white figure to transmit three separate pictures simultaneously in the three primary colors. Since this is not an acceptable solution, color information has to be contained within the 8 MHz channel allowed for black-and-white transmissions, which becomes an extremely complicated subject and virtually impossible to describe in simple terms. Strangely enough, however, it does simplify the other problem—the essential requirement that a color television should also be able to receive black-and-white transmissions in black and white. The broadcast stations still have the opposite problem of ensuring that color transmissions can be received on black-and-white sets in black-and-white!

The conventional color TV tube is made with three guns, one for each color—red, green, and blue; with each dot on the screen formed by separate red, green, and blue phosphors arranged in a triangle. The picture is thus scanned by a triangle of beams converging on each triangle of dots at the same rate as in a black-and-white picture. The resulting sharpness of the color picture depends primarily on the accuracy of convergence, and on some tubes may vary noticeably from center to edge and/or top to bottom. This may be a limitation of that particular design of tube and associated circuitry, or merely a matter of convergence adjustment (which is usually factory-set and can be quite complex). There are improvements in this respect in the case of some modern tubes; e.g., simplifying covergence problems by using in-line guns and color spots.

23
Microprocessors

The years 1939–45 saw the development of analog and digital computing techniques, and, towards the end of that era, the first appearance of electronic computers based on tubes and relays. The years 1948–50 saw digital computers established using tubes, and—more significantly—the development of the transistor.

Ten years later (1960), printed circuit boards first appeared, and also the first small-scale monolithic integrated circuits and hybrid integrated circuits. Transitional computer circuits took over from tubes. Medium-scale integrated circuits (MSI) appeared in 1965, and large scale integrated circuits (LSI) in 1970. Throughout this period of rapid development of ICs, many aspects of digital computing were further extended, culminating in the appearance of the first micro-miniaturized computer, or microprocessor, in 1971. From that date, there has been intensive development of digital integrated circuits in micro-miniature form through DTL to TTL to MOSFET and CMOS, etc. Throughout this period, the capabilities of microprocessors have continued to be improved, with, most significant of all, a fall in prices.

Essentially, the microprocessor is a digital computer in micro-miniaturized form, but not necessarily with the full capabilities of a conventional digital computer. One of its main applications, in fact, is a Programmable Logic Controller (PLC) for various industrial applications. Within the last five years or so, upwards of 60 different PLC systems have appeared, designed for industrial use, as well as others with more open capabilities. Each is associated with its own peripheral devices and associated software (i.e., programming devices).

Originally, PLCs were designed as one-bit processors, using discrete components. Today, they are invariably based on microprocessors, or, in some cases, combinations of both a microprocessor and a one-bit processor. Some of the more recently introduced types incorporate dual-language processors based on bit-slice technology.

One of the most important features of microprocessor is its size—not its physical size, but the length of the data word it operates on and the number of words its memory can store. Microprocessor language is measured by the number of bit per word, a *bit* being a *binary digit*. Common microprocessor word lengths are 4, 8, 12, and 16 bits. An 8-bit data word is by far the most common, and is given a special name—a *byte*.

Because there are only two possible combinations for one bit, it follows that the total number of combinations possible in a binary word in a given length is 2 raised to the Nth power, where N is the number of bits in a word. Thus, for an 8-bit word, the total number of combinations is 2^8-256.

As one measure of microprocessor size is the length of its word, this reflects on the size of the memory. The memory must be able to store a given number of words of this length. For example, a byte-oriented microprocessor with a memory that can store up to 10 words has 80 bits of storage capacity in the memory. It is generally assumed that a 4-bit microprocessor is accompanied by a memory storing 4-bit words, and a 16-bit microprocessor with 16-bit words of memory.

It follows, therefore, that memory size is measured by the number of words it may store. Often, the IC which is referred to as a microprocessor has little or no memory; the memory for the unit is contained in other ICs.

The maximum memory capacity of a PLC system depends on the addressing capability. But, in practice, the maximum expandability is related to the maximum physical number of inputs and outputs, and also of the complexity of control algorithms. A rule of thumb for calculating memory requirements is: 10–15 instructions (or commands) per one output on the average application for sequential control, with few arithmetic, timing, or counting functions. For applications with a more sophisticated control algorithm, 15–20 instructions per output may be required. You have to consider more memory space if several programs are to be stored simultaneously, which are selectable by a manual operation mode switch, for example, for frequently changing production at one machine. The maximum memory capacity of PLCs on the market ranges from 256 words (one word corresponds to one instruction) to 1600 words (commonly expressed as 16K) and more. Memory systems are modular and expandable from a minimum "starter set" of ¼K in increments of ¼K, 1K, and 4K.

In simple form, the microprocessor comprises three basic parts: the central processing unit (CPU), memory, and the I/O devices. A microprocessor always contains a CPU, and in some instances, memory as well as an I/O device. The CPU has the ability to send (address) information to either the memory of the I/O device (see Fig. 24-1).

Just as the memory must have an address before data may be transferred to or from it, so much the I/O devices. Normally, there is more than one input or output device on a system. Therefore, the CPU must decide which one it wishes to transfer data with, and this is done by addressing.

To execute a particular program, the programmer may set aside a certain area of the memory for program storage. Other areas of memory are be set aside for data storage, and these assignments may change for a different program. The Texas 510 PC, shown in schematic form in Fig. 23-1, illustrates the position of the microprocessor within the total package which includes memory storage, location area, image register (IR) and push-down stack (PDS).

All entries to the sequencer are made with a plug-in programmer. This can read out and modify all locations within the memory storage location area. When an entry is made, it is entered into and stored within this storage area. Timers and counters as well as series and parallel logic are contained therein.

The processor controls the Model 510 PC memory during programming and execution of the user program. Logic instructions from the programmer are entered into the storage area (user memory). At the start of each program scan, the processor places the status of the instruction in the register and transfers the status of the selected output to the output (Y) lines.

I/O modules are commonly available as plug-in cards or plug-on boxes in increments of 2, 4, 8, 16, and 32 lines per module. However, 8-stage modules and 16-stage modules seem to be the best buy. A broad variety of I/O cards with different signal-voltage levels are available from many manufacturers. Some types of I/O modules are: 5 Vdc Transistor-Transistor Logic (TTL); 24 Vdc; 48 Vdc; 120/24 Vdc; 24 Vac; and 120/24 Vac. In practical application, preference should be given to one standard signal voltage, so faulty I/O modules can be replaced by a spare I/O module of the same type.

Swapping I/O cards is a fast, sure, troubleshooting technique. Where possible, control elements and I/O modules of the same signal type should be used, which means an inexpensive stock of spare components. The output current load per line of various output cards ranges from 0.5A to 2A, but some PLCs on the market may have a problem — namely, not all outputs on a card can be energized

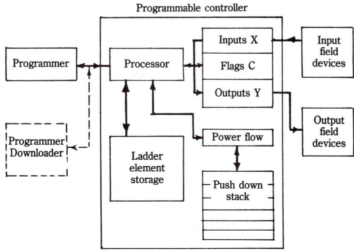

Fig. 23-1. Block diagram of Texas 510 programmable logic controller.

simultaneously because the card does not have the current-carrying ability to energize all outputs at once. The maximum number of inputs/outputs per system ranges from 32 for small, 128 for medium, and up to 4096 for large systems. However, at this point, it must be noticed that a large number of inputs/outputs, as well as corresponding large programs, may heavily reduce the response, or cycle, time of an application. The distributed systems concept may be more appropriate for a large and complex application.

Several larger PLCs have some capabilities or options which allow continuous process control with algorithms built-in for standard PID (Proportional-Integral-Differential) controllers with analog inputs and outputs. The combination of logic control and analog loop control means that these PLCs can be used for batch or continuous processing applications; however, they are not able to completely replace typical process-loop controllers. Usually, loop controllers are built as plug-in or plug-on modules for extended PLC systems. Optional available A/D (Analogue-to-Digital Converters) accept, respectively, supply signals of 4-20 mA or 0-5/0-10 Vdc. The signal resolution is rather low. Precise measurements are not possible at typically three-digit BCD (Binary Coded Decimal) value.

Counter and timer functions are indispensable tools of a PLC system. Nominally, up to 64 internal counters or timers are built into medium to large-scale PLCs. The time base is generated through a quartz oscillator clock that can commonly deliver three different time standards: 0.1 s, 1.0 s, and 1.0 min. Three-digit cascading up-and-down counters and timers provide convenient tools for a wide range of applications. For fast counting applications, such as positioning or angle-indicating transducers, separate fast counter cards are necessary. A critical specification for using internal counters is the counting frequency under the worst-case timing conditions, because the actual count-rate depends very much on how the program is structured; therefore, special attention must be paid to timing-related problems.

24
Batteries,
Power Supplies,
and Chargers

Virtually all portable electrical/electronic equipment acquires power from some type of battery. Batteries can be divided into two main groups: primary batteries, where the electrochemical action is irreversible (once the battery has been discharged it cannot be reenergized); and secondary batteries, where the electrochemical action is reversible (they can be charged and discharged repeatedly).

Primary batteries are popularly called dry batteries; and secondary batteries are called storage batteries. These descriptions are not strictly correct, but they are convenient and widely accepted. In fact, all primary batteries have some form of "wet" electrolyte (usually in the form of a paste or jelly); and many secondary batteries may have so-called "dry" cells (implying the use of a non-liquid electrolyte). And just to show how general classifications cannot always be strictly correct, some types of primary (non-rechargeable) battery systems are, in practice, rechargeable.

DRY BATTERIES (PRIMARY BATTERIES)

A battery is made up of one or more individual cells. Each cell develops a specific nominal voltage, depending on the battery system. To build a battery with a higher voltage than that given by a single cell, two or more cells are connected in series.

Choice of the best systems is dependent on cost and utilization of the battery. Carbon-zinc dry batteries are by far the most popular because they are relatively cheap and readily available in a wide range of voltages and sizes. (The size governs the capacity of the battery, or the amount of electrical energy it can store.)

SECONDARY BATTERIES

The familiar lead-acid battery was widely used in the early days of radio as a low-voltage battery. The only type of rechargeable battery which has a significant application in present-day electronics is the modern nickel-cadmium battery. It is the one type of secondary battery system in which "gassing" can be eliminated on charging, so it can be constructed in fully sealed-cell form (although many types are, in fact, constructed with resealing vents as a precaution).

Nickel-cadmium batteries offer numerous advantages — no deterioration during storage in either charged of discharged state (except that a charged cell suffers a loss of about 20 percent of its capacity a month); charge/recharge cycle life of a least several hundred and possibly thousands of charges (depending on actual use); suitabliity for high discharge rates (and high charge rates with vented cells); robustness; wide operating temperature range ($-40°$ to $+60°$ C.); and suitability for operating in almost any environment.

Disadvantages are high initial cost (although this is generally recoverable in long cycling life). and the fact that the nnominal voltage per cell is only 1.2 volts. However, the discharge characteristics are substantially flat.

USING BATTERIES

To increase the voltage of a battery, increase the number of cells connected in series to make up the battery. For a battery of given voltage:

$$\text{Number of cells required} = \frac{\text{REQUIRED BATTERY VOLTAGE}}{\text{VOLTS PER CELL}}$$

If the number of cells so calculated is not a whole number, use the next whole number up. For example:

Battery voltage required is 9 volts
Cells to be used are nickel-cadmium
Volts per cell is 1.2

$$\text{Number of cells required} = \frac{9}{1.2} = 7.5 \text{ cells}$$

Therefore, make up the battery from 8 cells connected in series. (The actual battery voltage is then $8 \times 1.2 = 9.6$ volts. If necessary, the additional voltage can always be dropped in a circuit by using a dropping resistor.)

To increase the capacity of a battery, connect two (or more) batteries of the required voltage in parallel. Two batteries connected in parallel halve the current drain from each battery, thus doubling the capacity. Basically, in fact, the capacity of the original battery is multiplied by the number of similar batteries connected in parallel.

OTHER DC POWER SOURCES

The application of a step-down transformer associated with a bridge rectifier and a smoothing capacitor to provide a low voltage dc supply from an ac mains supply has already been described in Fig. 8-5 Chapter 8. Rather more sophisticated circuits may be used where it is desirable to ensure a stable dc voltage; e.g., for operating an FM transistor radio from the ac mains instead of a battery.

A circuit of this type is shown in Fig. 26-1, the component values specified giving a stabilized dc output of 6 volts from 120 V AC. The bridge rectifier following the transformer provides full wave rectification, smoothed by capacitor C1 in the conventional manner.

The input to output voltage is dropped across transistor Q1. The emitter voltage of transistor Q2 is set by the Zener diode at 2.7 volts. The output voltage is divided by R4, R5 and when the voltage across R5 is about 3.2 volts, Q2 begins

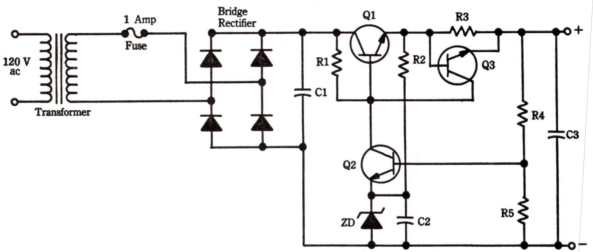

Fig. 24-1. Stabilized output dc charger operating from 120VAC power. Components are:

$$R1 = 680\ ohms$$
$$R2 = 820\ ohms$$
$$R3 = 1\ ohm$$
$$R4 = 39\ ohms\ for\ 6\ volts\ dc\ out$$
$$180\ ohms\ for\ 7.5\ volts\ dc\ out$$
$$R5 = 560\ ohms$$
$$C1 = 1000\ microfarad\quad 330\ ohms\ for\ 9\ volts\ dc\ out$$
$$C2 = 10\ microfarad$$
$$C3 = 0.01\ microfarad$$
$$T = 120/15\ volt\ transformer$$
$$BR = bridge\ rectifier$$
$$Q1 = SK3190$$
$$Q2 = SK3444$$
$$Q3 = SK3444$$
$$ZD = Zener\ diode - SK2V7$$

to conduct. This diverts some of the current flowing through R1 into the base of Q1 so that Q1 starts to turn off. Thus, since the base current, and the voltage drop across the collector-emitter junction of Q1, is controlled by Q2, the output voltage is stopped from going any higher than the design voltage.

Conversely, if a heavy load is applied to the output it tends to cause a drop in output voltage and so also the voltage on the base of Q2 tends to fall. The effect of this is that Q2 starts to turn off, allowing more current to flow into the base of Q1 which turns on to maintain the output voltage.

Voltage stabilization is maintained until the output current rises to the order of 400-500 mA. At this point, the voltage across R3 becomes greater than the turn-on voltage of Q3, which starts to conduct. This taps current from the base of Q1, causing Q1 to start to turn off, reducing the output voltage, so that the current does not rise any further. In other words the circuit is automatically protected against overload, even down to short circuit conditions. In the latter case, the voltage will fall to almost zero, with the current still maintained at 400 – 500 milliamps. The capacitors C2 and C3 are not strictly necessary, but are additional smoothing components.

The circuit can be adapted to provide a number of different dc output voltages, selectable by switching. To do this, resistor R4 is replaced by a chain of resistors

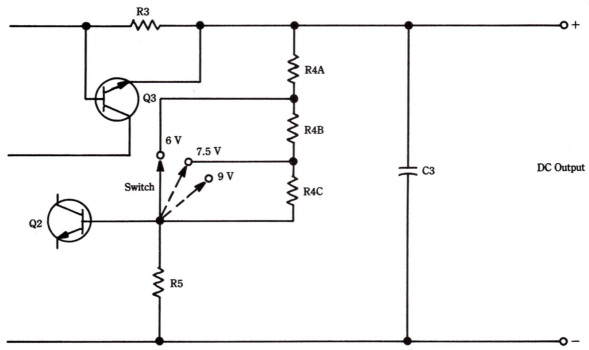

Fig. 24-2. Switching circuit for altering dc output voltage.

R4A = 39 ohms
R4B = 150 ohms
R4C = 150 ohms

R4A, R4B, R4C, as in Fig. 24-2. The values given, together with the previous circuit component values, provide selectable outputs of 6 volts, or 9 volts, with voltage stabilized in each case up to a maximum current drain of 400–500 milliamps.

BATTERY CHARGERS

Either a bridge rectifier circuit, or the voltage-stabilized circuit just described, can also be used for battery charging. In this case, smoothing is not so important, as the presence of a certain amount of ripple in the dc is held to be beneficial for charging. Normally, however, at least one smoothing capacitor would be desirable in the charger circuit.

Since it is not always evident whether a charger is working or not, an indicator lamp or ammeter is normally desirable in a charger circuit. A lamp merely indicates that the charger is on and the output circuit is working. It can be tapped directly across the circuit at any point. The preferred form of lamp is an LED since this draws minimal current, although a small filament bulb will do as well. An LED needs to be associated with a ballast resistor to drop the necessary voltage at this point; a filament bulb does not, but a resistor is needed to work as a voltage dropper if a 6-volt bulb is used in this circuit (see Fig. 24-3). Note that an indicator lamp on the mains side of the transformer, or on the secondary side

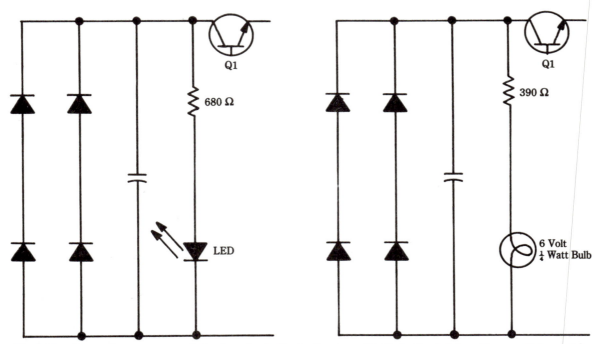

Fig. 24-3. Alternative arrangements for charging indicator lamps.   A bulb of appropriate voltage could be used in one of the output leads without a dropping resistor.

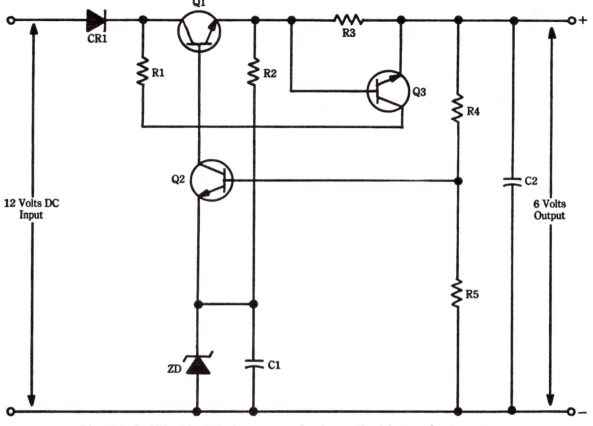

Fig. 24-4. Stabilized 6 volt dc charger operating from a 12 volt battery. Components are:

$R1 = 680\ ohms$
$R2 = 820\ ohms$
$R3 = 1\ ohm$
$R4 = 39\ ohms$
$R5 = 560\ ohms$
$C1 = 10\ microfarads$
$C2 = 0.01\ microfarads$
$Q1 = SK3190$
$Q2 = SK3444$
$Q3 = SK3444$
$ZD = Zener\ diode - SK2V7$
$CR1 = 1N4001\ (or\ equivalent)$

between the transformer and the bridge rectifier, would not necessarily confirm that the output was working with an output load connected.

In the case of a meter indicator, this would simply be an ammeter (or milliam-meter, as appropriate) connected in series in one or another of the output lines.

DC INPUT CHARGERS

There is also a call for chargers which can charge low voltage batteries direct from another battery, such as a 12-volt car battery. In this case, since the input is dc, a transformer cannot be used to set the required voltage, nor is a rectifier necessary.

Figure 24-4 shows a charger circuit designed to provide a stabilized 6-volt dc output (charging voltage) from a 12-volt input supply. Essentially, it is the same as that of Fig. 24-1 without the transformer and rectifier, but a diode is included to protect the transistors in the circuit against reverse voltages. Working of the circuit is the same as that described previously, with automatic short-circuit protection. Like the previous mains circuit, too, it can be adapted to provide a range of output voltages, using exactly the same values for the chain of resistors as in Fig. 24-2.

25
High-Voltage Power Supplies

The basic way to obtain a high-voltage supply is to step up an ac mains supply via a transformer. At the same time, the transformer can be tapped, or provided with separate windings, to produce any other lower or intermediate voltages which may be required. Voltage step-up or step-down, using a transformer, is possible only with an alternating-current input. The resulting output is also ac, from which it follows that further components are required in a power supply to provide stepped-up or -down direct-current voltages, such as required for the anode of a tube. Basically, this involves rectification of the transformed voltage, with the addition of smoothing, if necessary, to remove any remaining ripple, in the dc output.

Voltage regulation may also be necessary, even if it is only aimed at limiting the value of transient voltages which may be introduced in the power-supply circuit. In that case, we are concerned with the peak inverse voltages (piv) which may be introduced in the power-supply circuit, affecting the loading of the components. Voltage regulation itself can be expressed as a percentage:

$$\text{regulation (\%)} = \frac{100(\text{E1-E2})}{\text{E2}}$$

E1 is the no-load voltage (no current flowing in the load circuit), and E2 is the full load voltage (rated current flowing in load circuit).

Three basic rectifier circuits are shown in Fig. 25-1. A single diode provides

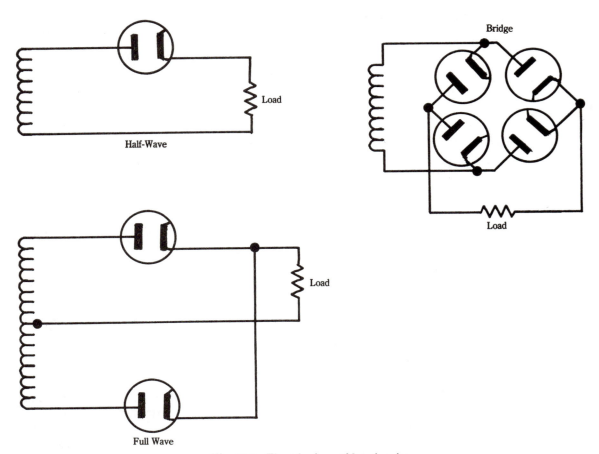

Fig. 25-1. Three basic rectifier circuits.

half-wave rectification. Two diodes can provide full-wave rectification, with the circuit completed through the transformer center tap. Alternatively, the bridge type circuit can be used for full-wave rectification.

Either tubes (diodes) or metal rectifiers can be used in such circuits. Metal rectifiers require no heater supply, but have to be fitted with cooling fins to dissipate the heat generated by their relatively high forward resistance. Tubes also get hot, and both need plenty of space within the cabinet, and good ventilation. Power supplies of these types, therefore, tend to be heavy and bulky.

Silicon power diodes are generally preferred to tubes or metal rectifiers. They can be produced in virtually miniature size, require no heater current, and have relatively low heating (and thus much higher efficiency), because of their very low forward resistance. While this ltter feature is highly desirable, it does also emphasize the potential weakness of the silicon diode. High voltage surges can develop which may destroy the diode. This is because of the relatively low piv values such diodes can withstand. Unfortunately, too, silicon diodes also tend to fail in a shorted condition, rather than open, so that failure of one diode in a series could readily cause the remainder to fail as well.

Series connection of silicon diodes is generally necessary to realize the piv rating required. This is determined by the piv likely to be developed by the rectifier circuit. In the case of a single diode circuit, the piv across the diode is approximately 1.4 times the ac voltage across the transformer coil. The center-tap circuit yields a piv of about 2.8 times the ac voltage across each half of the transformer coil. The bridge circuit again yields about 1.4 times the voltage across the coil.

The required rating can be built up by connecting as many diodes in series as necessary to factor their individual rating by 2, 3, 4 times, etc., allowing a suitable margin of safety. This, however, is only valid if the diodes are exactly matched in characteristics (particularly their reverse resistance). This is unlikely in practice, and so equalizing resistors are normally connected across each diode—Fig. 25-2. Alternatively, equalizing capacitors may be used in some circuits. Both configurations, incidentally, also act as transient suppressors to protect the diodes against surges of high current. Since capacitors are more effective in this respect, resistors and capacitors may be used in series across each diode as equalizing/damping devices. Further protection may also be incorporated in the rectifier circuit by including a fuse to open-circuit a chain of diodes in the event of overload, or failure of one of the diodes.

One other precaution which may be necessary with silicon diodes is to balance their rating against temperature. Although they do not generate much heat themselves, their performance is temperature-dependent, and the maximum rating applies with a temperature limit. If they are to be worked at a higher ambient temperature, derating their performance is necessary. Temperatures for a maximum current rating may range from as low as 25°C to as high as 70°C, depending on type and manufacture. Derating, typically, is of the order of 10 percent per 10°C temperature rise above the rated temperature.

FILTERS

The output from a rectifier circuit is pulsating dc. To render this in the form of smooth dc, filtering must be applied. While this may not be strictly necessary for tube operation, it is absolutely necessary to eliminate (or at least reduce) the hum content of the power supply applied to various stages of a transmitter or receiver circuit.

Effective smoothing of the supply is readily achieved by means of a capacitor-input filter, which may be either single-section or two- section—Fig. 25-3. The

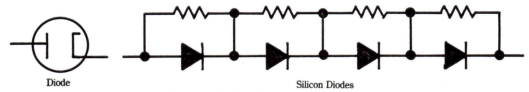

Diode   Silicon Diodes

Fig. 25-2. Diodes with equalizing resistors.

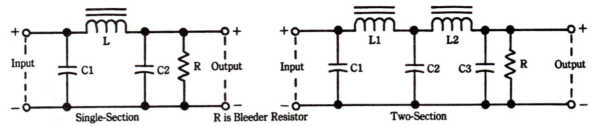

Single-Section   R is Bleeder Resistor   Two-Section

Fig. 25-3. Single and two-section smoothing filters.

single-section filter is generally adequate for radio transmitters, but the two-section circuit is preferable for radio receivers. The addition of a bleeder resistor is generally recommended, to discharge the capacitors when the power supply is not in use. The value of the bleeder resistance should be chosen so that it draws 10 percent or less of the rated output current of the supply. (It can be calculted directly as 1000E/I ohms, where E is the output voltage, and I is the load current in milliamps.)

The ripple voltage remaining is governed by the values of the capacitors and inductance. Typical values are $8\ \mu F$ for the capacitors (although C1 can be reduced to $4\ \mu F$ in the two-section circuit), with an inductance of 20 to 30 henries. Ripple voltage gets smaller as capacitance and inductance are made larger. Few problems are imposed in matching component values, and satisfactory smoothing is readily obtained. Capacitor-input filter circuit, however, exhibit poor voltage-regulation properties when used with varying loads.

The choke-input filter provides better voltage regulation, but less effective smoothing. Again, it can be single-section or two-section—Fig. 25-4. The two-section circuit is generally superior as regards smoothing. Note again the use of a bleeder resistor to discharge the capacitor(s) when the power supply is not in use.

The first indictance can, with advantage, be of the swinging choke type—that is, having swinging characteristics over a range of about 5 to 20 henries over the full output current range. The highest value then applies when there is no output load on the power supply other than the bleeder resistor. The second choke should then have a constant inductance of 10 to 20 henries with varying dc load currents.

With this type of circuit, it is possible to use capacitors with lower rated voltage than those necessary for a capacitor-input filter (which have to have a rating higher than the peak transformer voltage). However, a similar high-volt-

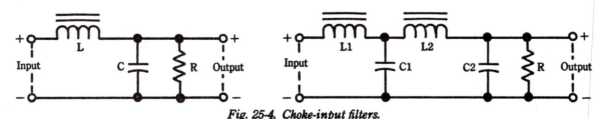

Fig. 25-4. Choke-input filters.

age rating is usually advised, as in the event of failure of the bleeder resistor the voltages would rise to these peak figures.

OUTPUT VOLTAGE

Basically, the dc output voltage is about 0.9 times the ac voltage across the transformer secondary in the case of a single diode or bridge circuit; and about 0.45 times the ac voltage across the transformer secondary in the case of the bridge circuit. With capacitor-input filters, the secondary rms voltage required is thus 1/0.9 or 1.1 times the required dc output voltage, to allow for voltage drops in the rectifier and filter circuits, and in the transformer itself. In the case of a center-tapped circuit, this voltage must be developed across each side of the secondary center tap.

With a choke-input filter circuit following the rectifier, the required transformer secondary voltage can be calculated directly from:

$$E = 1.1 \left(E_o + \frac{1(R1 + R2)}{1000} + E_r \right)$$

where:

E = full load rms secondary voltage

E_o = required dc output voltage (The open circuit voltage will usually be anything from 5 to 10 percent higher.)

E_r = voltage drop in the rectifier

$R1, R2$ = resistance in filter chokes

VOLTAGE STABILIZATION

A basic method of obtaining voltage stabilization is by the use of a voltage-regulating tube in series with a limiting resistor, as shown in Fig. 25-5. The initial (unregulated) voltage needs to be higher than the starting voltage of the tube, which is usually about 30 percent higher than the operating voltage. The value of the limiting resistor is chosen to just pass the maximum tube current when there is no load current. With load added, the tube can then work down to its minimum current condition. Within this range the voltage drop of the tube is constant, thus providing a point for tapping off a stabilized voltage. Voltage regulation better than 10 percent can readily be achieved; and with the tubes in series, stabilization is further improved down to about 1 percent. The use of two tubes in series also enables two different values of regulated voltage to be tapped, one from each tube.

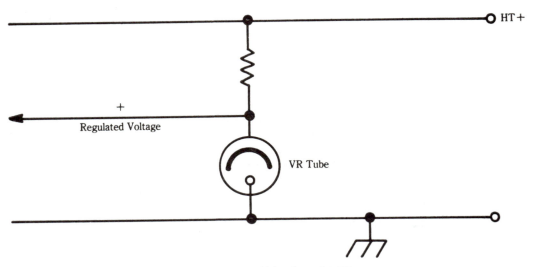

Fig. 25-5. Voltage stabilization with VR tube.

Figure 25-6 shows how Zener diodes can also be used to stabilize a high-voltage supply obtained from a transformer. The low-voltage Zener diodes (Z1 and Z2) are simply connected in back-to-back configuration across a low-voltage winding on the transformer.

BIAS VOLTAGES

Bias-supply requirements are basically a fixed voltage of the required value to set the operating point of a tube. The output should be well-filtered, and capacitor-input filters are commonly preferred. A bleeder resister is effective as a

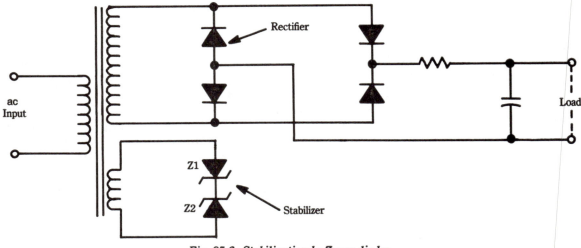

Fig. 25-6. Stabilization by Zener diodes.

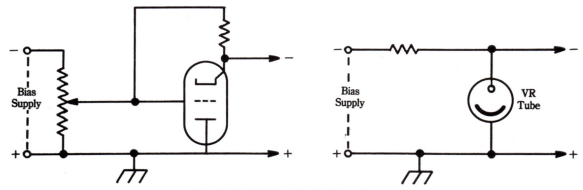

Fig. 25-7. Stabilization by bias voltage.

voltage regulator since it provides a dc path from the grid to the cathode of the tube being biased. However, to be really effective, this needs a low resistance value so that the current flowing through the bleeder resistor is several times the maximum grid current to be expected, which is wasteful of power.

In particular cases, therefore, it may be expedient to adopt more efficient methods of bias-voltage stabilization. Two such stabilizing circuits are shown in Fig. 25-7. One uses a triode as a regulator, and the other a VR tube. The latter is only applicable where the voltage and current ratings of the tubes permit their application.

VOLTAGE DIVIDERS

The conventional type of voltage divider is based on the circuit shown in Fig. 25-8. Basically, it comprises a series of resistors (or a resistor with a series of tapping points), from which voltages lower than the input voltage can be drawn

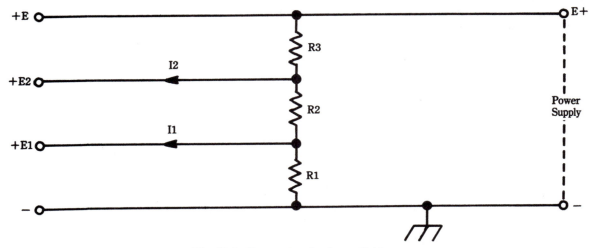

Fig. 25-8. Conventional voltage divider.

by connecting to an appropriate tap. The end resistor is only as a bleeder, carrying a bleeder current which is normally 10 percent or less of the total load current. The values of resistors required then follow from:

$$R1 = \frac{EI}{I_b}$$

$$R2 = \frac{E2 - E1}{I_b + I_1}$$

$$R3 = \frac{E - E2}{I_b + I_1 + I_2}$$

Voltage regulation is very poor with voltage dividers of this type because the voltage taken from any tap depends on the current drawn from the tap (and will thus vary with varying load). Thus, while they are suitable for constant-load applications, additional voltage regulation would have to be applied for stabilization with varying loads.

VOLTAGE MULTIPLIERS

Rectifiers can also be used as voltage-multipliers, in integer factors — a feature which can often be used to advantage. It is possible, for example, to accept an ac input direct into a rectifier circuit, without having to employ a transformer, and obtain both rectification and voltage doubling. Such a circuit is shown in Fig. 25-9. Each capacitor is charged separately to the same dc voltage from the two diodes and then discharged in series into the same load circuit (thus doubling the dc output voltage obtained).

Figure 25-10 shows an extension of this principle, utilizing four diodes. The output from this circuit provides both voltage doubling and voltage quadrupling.

As with voltage dividers, voltage multipliers tend to offer poor voltage regulation, although this is less marked with silicon diodes as compared with diode tubes and metal rectifiers.

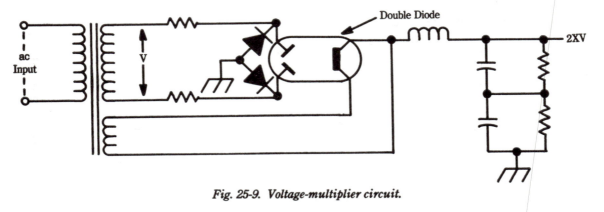

Fig. 25-9. Voltage-multiplier circuit.

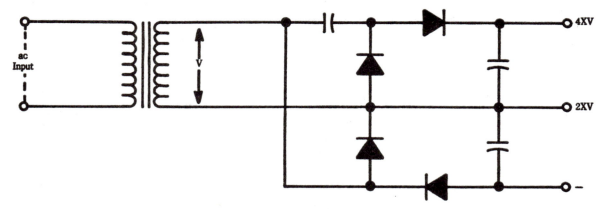

Fig. 25-10. Voltage-multiplier circuit using diodes.

VARIABLE-VOLTAGE SUPPLIES

A simple type of variable-voltage supply for use with a constant-voltage power supply is shown in Fig. 25-11. This circuit eliminates series resistors as a source of voltage drop and, as a consequence, maintains a substantially constant source impedance. Voltage regulation is also provided, as well as voltage variation via the variable resistor, although the degree of stabilization deteriorates with increasing voltage output. It is, however, another example of how simple circuits can often be used to provide solutions to particular requirements in transmitter and/or receiver circuits.

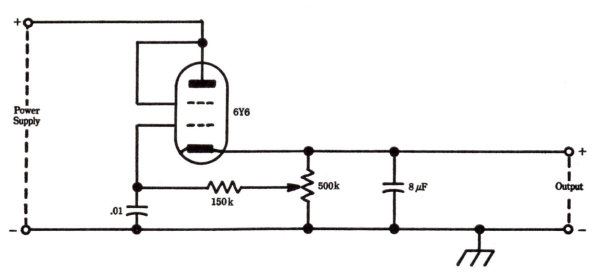

Fig. 25-11. Variable voltage supply.

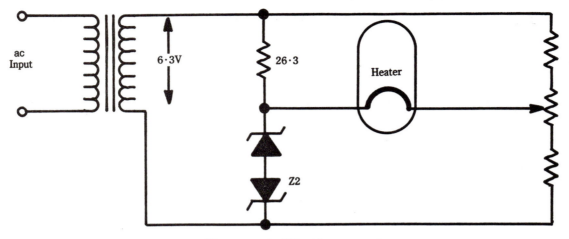

Fig. 25-12. Stabilized heater supply.

STABILIZED TUBE HEATER SUPPLIES

The heater supply for tubes tends to be regarded as non-critical, and conveniently supplied direct from a separate low-voltage coil on the power transformer, without rectification. As a minimum precaution, it is generally desirable to use separate heater supplies (e.g., separate transformer coils) for oscillator tubes, and voltage stabilization may well be considered as a method of further improving the overall stability of the stage(s) involved.

A simple circuit which offers considerable possibilities in this respect is shown in Fig. 25-12, employing two Zener diodes in back-to-back bridge circuit configuration. The potentiometer acts as a trimmer to set up the circuit, its value being about 20 percent of the total resistance value of the lower arm of the bridge. Voltage stabilization of better than 1 percent is claimed for this circuit, with a transformer voltage change of up to 13 percent.

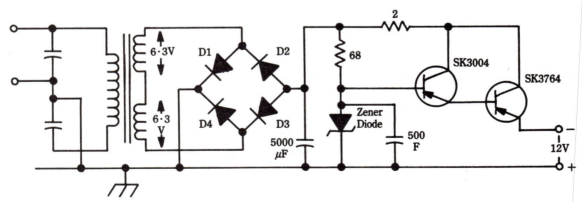

Fig. 25-13. Transistor power supply.

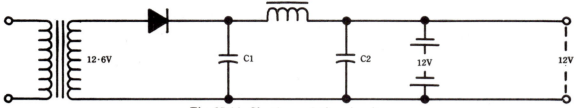

Fig. 25-14. Simple regulation circuit.

TRANSISTOR POWER SUPPLIES

Transistor circuits require only low voltages and thus considerably simplify power supply requirements, particularly as only a single voltage is usually required. They may, however, be fed from an ac supply, in which case, similar requirements apply as regards rectification and smoothing following the transformer. For voltage stabilization, a Zener diode is normally employed (the Zener diode is virtually the counterpart of the VR tube in higher voltage circuits).

A typical modern transistor power supply circuit is shown in Fig. 25-13, which is also notable for incorporating electronic smoothing. There are numerous variations on a similar theme but, in general, shunt regulation is taking preference over series regulation, as this will permit the output to be short-circuited without damage.

A very much simpler system is shown in Fig. 25-14 which merely uses half-wave rectification followed by smoothing, and a battery of the same voltage as the dc output floating across the output. This battery provides extremely good stabilization and at the same time can also act as a ripple filter. Capacitor C2, in fact, is not really necessary. Basically, the battery provides an additional source of power to combat voltage drop under load. A similar system of floating a battery across the output can equally well be applied to a full-wave rectifier output. Zener diode stabilization can also be added, if necessary, for an even higher degree of stabilization.

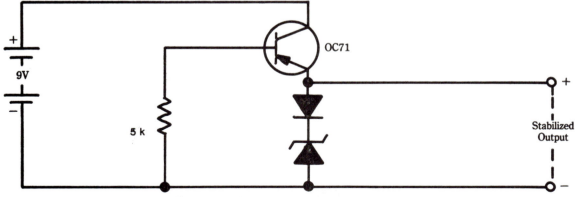

Fig. 25-15. Simple low-loss stabilizing circuit.

Stabilization is less readily provided across a direct battery feed to a transistor circuit since conventional methods of stabilization using Zener diodes and resistors almost inevitably mean a large increase in current drain, further loading the batteries. Various ingenious solutions have been proposed to combat this, such as the use of current-limiting circuits (which also safeguard transistors against overload). Figure 25-15 shows a simple low-loss stabilizing circuit, based around the use of a transistor as a constant current device, which can readily be extended to two stages if necessary.

Appendix:
Symbols and Equations

The following equations are used often in the field of electronics. In addition to equations discussed in the previous text, this section also contains many other equations for future reference.

SYMBOLS USED

Symbol	Meaning
A	Length of the side adjacent to θ in the right triangle, in same units as the other sides
B	Susceptance (measured in seimens or mhos); the reciprocal of reactance
C	Capacitance (measured in farads); Celsius temperature
D	Dissipation factor; reciprocal of storage factor Q
d	Thickness of the dielectric material in a capacitor (measured in centimeters)
dB	Decibel; the ratio between two amounts of power
E	Electromotive force (measured in volts)
F	Temperature (measured in degrees Fahrenheit)
f	Frequency (measured in hertz)
G	Conductance (measured in siemens or mhos)
H	Length of the hypotenuse in a right triangle, in same units as the other sides

I	Current, in amperes
J	Energy, work, or quantity of heat (measured in joules)
K	Coupling coefficient, dielectric constant, or temperature in kelvins
L	Inductance (measured in henries)
M	Mutual inductance (measured in henries)
N	General symbol for numbers
O	Length of the side opposite to θ in a right triangle, in same units as the other sides
P	Power (measured in watts)
p.f.	Power factor
Q	Quality of an inductor, or quantity of electricity stored (measured in coulombs)
R	Resistance (measured in ohms)
S	Area of one plate of a capacitor (measured in square centimeters)
X	Reactance (measured in ohms); measure of opposition of a circuit or component to an alternating current.
X	Capacitive reactance (measured in ohms)
X	Inductive reactance (measured in ohms)
Y	Admittance (measured in siemens or mhos), the reciprocal of impedance; the lack of opposition to the flow of alternating current in a reactive circuit
Z	Impedance (measured in ohms), the reciprocal of admittance; the opposition to the flow of alternating current in a reactive circuit
δ	90-θ degrees
θ	Phase angle (measured in degrees); in a right triangle, simply an angle
λ	Wavelength (measured in meters)
π	3.1416 . . .
ω_c	Cutoff frequency

ADMITTANCE

(1) $Y = \dfrac{1}{\sqrt{R^2 + X^2}}$

(2) $Y = \dfrac{1}{Z}$

(3) $Y = \sqrt{G^2 + B^2}$

AVERAGE VALUE

(1) Average value = 0.637 (peak value)

(2) Average value = 0.900 (R.M.S. value)

CAPACITANCE

(1) Capacitors in parallel:

$$C_{TOTAL} = C_1 + C_2 + C_3 \ldots \text{etc.}$$

(2) Capacitors in series:

$$C_{TOTAL} = \cfrac{1}{\cfrac{1}{C_1} + \cfrac{1}{C_2} + \cfrac{1}{C_3} \cdots \text{etc.}}$$

(3) Two capacitors in series:

$$C_{TOTAL} = \frac{C_1 C_2}{C_1 + C_2}$$

(4) Capacitance of a capacitor:

$$C = 0.0885 \frac{KS(N-1)}{d}$$

(5) Quantity of electricity stored:

$$Q = CE$$

CONDUCTANCE

(1) $G = \dfrac{1}{R}$

(2) $G = \dfrac{I}{E}$

(3) $G_{TOTAL} = G_1 + G_2 + G_3 \ldots$ etc. (Resistors in parallel)

(4) $I_{TOTAL} = EG_{TOTAL}$

COSECANT

(1) $\csc \ \theta = \dfrac{H}{O}$

(2) $\csc \ \theta = \sec (90-\theta)$

(3) $\csc \ \theta = \dfrac{1}{\sin \theta}$

COSINE

(1) $\cos \theta = \dfrac{A}{H}$

(2) $\cos \theta = \sin (90 - \theta)$

(3) $\cos \theta = \dfrac{1}{\sec \theta}$

COTANGENT

(1) $\cot \theta = \dfrac{A}{O}$

(2) $\cot \theta = \tan (90 - \theta)$

(3) $\cot \theta = \dfrac{1}{\tan \theta}$

DECIBEL

(1) $dB = 10 \log \dfrac{P_1}{P_2}$

(2) $dB = 20 \log \dfrac{E_1}{E_2}$ Only if source and load impedance are equal

(3) $dB = 20 \log \dfrac{I_1}{I_2}$ Only if source and load impedance are equal

(4) $dB = 20 \log \dfrac{E_1 \sqrt{Z_2}}{E_2 \sqrt{Z_1}}$ Source and load impedances are unequal

(5) $dB = 20 \log \dfrac{I_1 \sqrt{Z_1}}{I_2 \sqrt{Z_2}}$ Source and load impedances are unequal

FIGURE OF MERIT

(1) $Q = \tan \theta$

(2) $Q = \dfrac{X}{R}$

FILTERS, ACTIVE

There are four basic filter types; high pass, low pass, bandpass, and band-stop. The following filter types are referred to as "constant-K" and are practical for most purposes.

Low-pass and High-pass

$$C = \dfrac{1}{\omega_c R} \quad L = \dfrac{R}{\omega_c}$$

where:

$C =$ capacitance in farads
$L =$ inductance in Henries
$R =$ nominal terminating resistance $= \sqrt{L/C}$
$\omega_c =$ cutoff frequency $= 2 \pi f_c = 6.28 \, f_c$

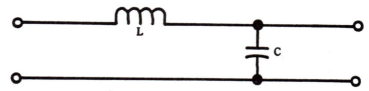

Fig. A-1. Low-pass filter circuit.

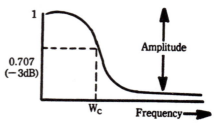

Fig. A-2. Low-pass filter-effecton frequency.

Band-pass

$$C_1 = \frac{\omega_2 - \omega_1}{R\omega_0^2} \qquad L_1 = \frac{R}{\omega_2 - \omega_1}$$

$$C_2 = \frac{1}{R(\omega_2 - \omega_1)} \qquad L_2 = \frac{R(\omega_2 - \omega_1)}{\omega_0^2}$$

where:

C_1 = Series capacitance in farads
C_2 = Shunt capacitance in farads
L_1 = Series inductance in henries
L_2 = Shunt inductance in henries
R = Nominal terminating resistance = $[\sqrt{L_1/C_2} = \sqrt{L_2/C_1}$
ω_0 = Midband frequency = $\dfrac{1}{(\sqrt{L_1\,C_1}} = \dfrac{1}{\sqrt{L_2\,C_2})} = 2\pi f_0 = 6.28\ f_0$
ω_1 = Lower cutoff frequency $\times$ 6.28
ω_2 = Upper cutoff frequency $\times$ 6.28

Band-stop

$$C_1 = \frac{1}{R(\omega_2 - \omega_1)} \qquad L_1 = \frac{R(\omega_2 - \omega_1)}{\omega_1\omega_2}$$

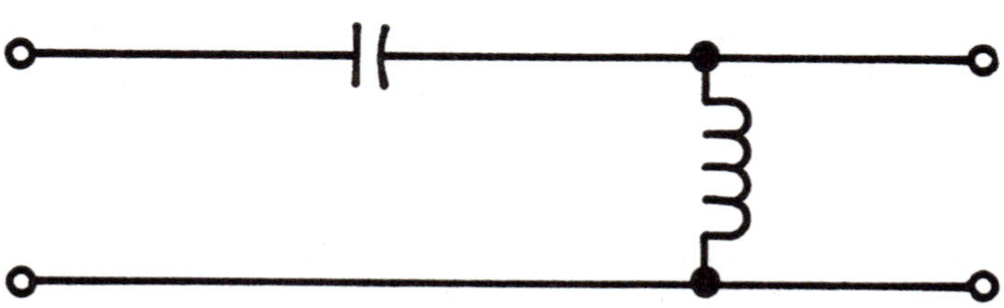

Fig. A-3. High-pass filter circuit.

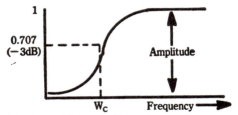

Fig. A-4. High-pass filter-effect on frequency.

$$C_2 = \frac{\omega_2 - \omega_1}{\omega_1 \, \omega_2 \, R} \qquad L_2 = \frac{R}{\omega_2 - \omega_1}$$

where:

$$\omega_o = \text{midband frequency} = (\sqrt{\omega_1 \omega_2} = 1/\sqrt{L_1 C_1} = 1/\sqrt{L_2 C_2})6.28$$

All other expressions are the same as band-pass.

FILTERS ACTIVE

Active filters incorporate an active device (transistor, operational amplifier, etc.) to replace the difficult to find inductors. Active filters are smaller and easier to modify for specific needs. They can also provide higher Q values than their passive counterparts. The following equations and tables are applicable to most IC operational amplifiers (including FET types).

Low-Pass Filters

Figure A-9 illustrates a common form of active low-pass filter. The value of C_1 is determined by dividing the desired cut-off frequency (fc) into 10. The result of this calculation is the value of C1 in microfarads. Next, multiply the value of C_1 with the desired fc and divide this product into 159. This result is the scale factor, needed to calculate the values of the remaining components from the following table:

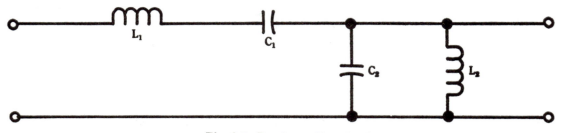

Fig. A-5. Band-pass filter circuit.

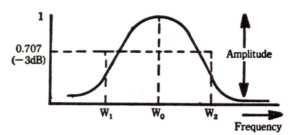

Fig. A-6. Band-pass filter-effect on frequency.

Component	For Gain of 2	For Gain of 10
C_2 (in μF)	0.150 × value of C_1	0.033 × value of C_1
R_1 (in KΩ)	1.612 × scale factor	1.021 × scale factor
R_2 (in KΩ)	3.223 × scale factor	10.211 × scale factor
R_3 (in KΩ)	2.068 × scale factor	2.968 × scale factor

Example:
Desired fc = 500 Hz; Gain = 2

$$C_1 = \frac{10}{500} = 0.02 \ \mu F$$

$$C_2 = (0.02)0.150 = .003 \ \mu F$$

$$\text{scale factor} = \frac{159}{f_c C_1} = \frac{159}{10} = 15.9$$

$$R_1 = (1.612)15.9 = 25.63 \ k\Omega$$

$$R_2 = (3.223)15.9 = 51.24 \ k\Omega$$

$$R_3 = (2.068)15.9 = 32.88 \ k\Omega$$

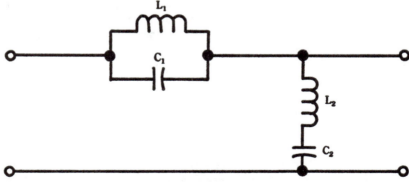

Fig. A-7. Band-stop filter circuit.

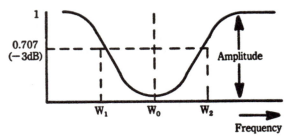

Fig. A-8. Band-stop filter-effect on frequency.

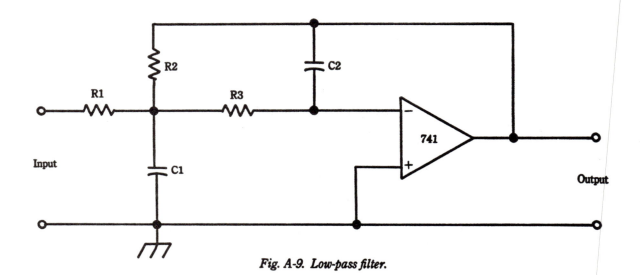

Fig. A-9. Low-pass filter.

High-Pass Filters

Figure A-10 illustrates a common form of active high-pass filter. The value of C_1 is determined by dividing the desired cutoff frequency (f_c) into 10. The result of this calculation is the value of C_1 in microfarads. Next, multiply the value of C_1 with the desired fc and divide this product into 159. This result is the scale factor. The scale factor is needed to calculate the values of the remaining components from the following table:

Component	For Gain of 2	For Gain of 10
C_2 (in μF)	0.500 × value of C_1	0.100 × value of C_1
C_3 (in μF)	1.000 × value of C_1	1.000 × value of C_1
R_1 (in kΩ)	0.566 × scale factor	0.673 × scale factor
R_2 (in kΩ)	3.536 × scale factor	14.849 × scale factor

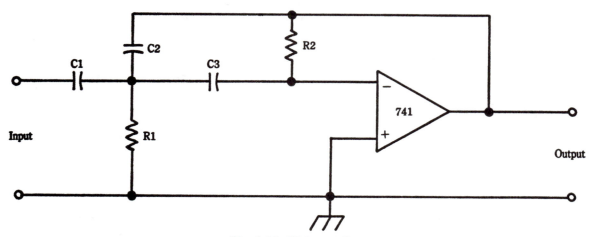

Fig. A-10. High-pass filter.

Example:
  Desired fc = 50 Hz; Gain = 2

$$C_1 = \frac{10}{500} = 0.02 \ \mu F$$

$$C_2 = (0.02)0.500 = 0.01 \ \mu F$$

$$C_3 = (0.02)1.000 = 0.02 \ \mu F$$

$$\text{scale factor} = \frac{159}{f_c C_1} = \frac{159}{10} = 15.9$$

$$R_1 = (0.566)15.9 = 8.99 \ k\Omega$$

$$R_2 = (3.536)15.9 = 56.22 \ k\Omega$$

Bandpass Filter

Figure A-11 illustrates a common form of active bandpass filter. The value of C_1 is determined by dividing the desired center frequency (fo) into 10. The result of this calculation is the value of C_1 in microfarads. Next, multiply the value of C_1 with the desired fo and divide this product into 159. The result is the scale factor, used to calculate the values of the remaining components from the following table:

Component	For Gain of 2	For Gain of 10
C_2 (in μF)	1.000 × value of C_1	2.000 × value of C_1
R_1 (in kΩ)	1.000 × scale factor	0.200 × scale factor
R_2 (in kΩ)	0.333 × scale factor	1.000 × scale factor
R_3 (in kΩ)	4.000 × scale factor	3.000 × scale factor

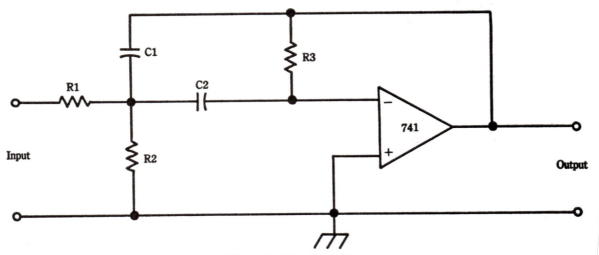

Fig. A-11. Band pass filter.

Example:
Desired $f_o = 500$ Hz; Gain = 10

$$C_1 = \frac{10}{500} = 0.02 \ \mu F$$

$$C_2 = (2.000)0.02 = 0.04 \ \mu F$$

$$\text{scale factor} = \frac{159}{f_o C_1} = \frac{159}{10} = 15.9$$

$$R_1 = (0.200)15.9 = 3.18 \ k\Omega$$

$$R_2 = (1.000)15.9 = 15.9 \ k\Omega$$

$$R_3 = (3.000)15.9 = 47.7 \ k\Omega$$

For a narrower bandpass, a higher Q value is required. The values of R_1, R_2, and R_3 can be adjusted by multiplying them by the factors given in the following table:

Desired Value of Q	For Gain of 2		For Gain of 10	
	R_1 and R_3	R_2	R_1 and R_3	R_2
4	2	0.400	2	0.105
6	3	0.258	3	0.061
8	4	0.189	4	0.044
10	5	0.153	5	0.034

Example:
Desire a Q of 8 from the previous bandpass calculations while maintaining the gain at 10.

$$R_1 = 3.18 \text{ k}\Omega \times 4 = 12.72 \text{ k}\Omega$$
$$R_2 = 15.9 \text{ k}\Omega \times 0.044 = 0.699 \text{ k}\Omega$$
$$R_3 = 47.7 \text{ k}\Omega \times 4 = 190.8 \text{ k}\Omega$$

Bandstop Filter (Band-Reject or Notch Filter)

Figure G-12 illustrates a common form of bandstop filter. The value of C_1 is determined by dividing the desired center frequency (f_o) into 10. The result of this calculation is the value of C_1 in microfarads. Next, multiply the value of C_1 with the desired f_o and divide this product into 159. The result is the scale factor. C_2's capacitance is twice that of C_1. For unity gain (gain of 1), the following table of multipliers can be used to obtain the values of the three resistors depending on the desired Q. Simply multiply the scale factor by the multipliers. The product will be in kilohms.

Desired Value of Q	R_1	R_2	R_3
1	0.500	2.000	0.400
2	0.250	4.000	0.235
3	0.167	6.000	0.162
4	0.125	8.000	0.123
5	0.100	10.000	0.099
6	0.083	12.000	0.083
7	0.071	14.000	0.071
8	0.063	16.000	0.062
9	0.056	18.000	0.055
10	0.050	20.000	0.050

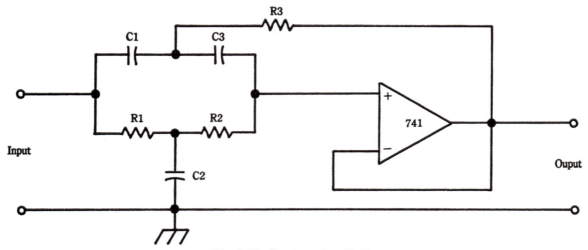

Fig. A-12. Bandstop (notch) filter.

Example:
  Desired $f_0 = 500$ Hz; $Q = 5$

$$C_1 = \frac{10}{500} = 0.02 \ \mu F$$

$$C_2 = 2(0.02 \ \mu F) = 0.04 \ \mu F$$

$$\text{scale factor} = \frac{159}{C_1 f_0} = \frac{159}{10} = 15.9$$

$$R_1 = (0.100)15.9 = 1.59 \ k\Omega$$

$$R_2(10.000)15.9 = 159 \ k\Omega$$

$$R_3 = (0.099)15.9 = 1.57 \ k\Omega$$

FREQUENCY

(1) $f = \dfrac{3 \times 10^8}{\lambda}$

(2) $f = \dfrac{1}{2\pi\sqrt{LC}}$

IMPEDANCE

(1) $Z = \sqrt{R^2 + X^2}$

(2) $Z = \sqrt{G^2 + B^2}$

(3) $Z = \dfrac{R}{\cos\theta}$

(4) $Z = \dfrac{X}{\sin\theta}$

(5) $Z = \dfrac{E}{I}$

(6) $Z = \dfrac{P}{I^2 \cos\theta}$

(7) $Z = \dfrac{E^2 \cos\theta}{P}$

INDUCTANCE

(1) Inductors in series:
$$L_{TOTAL} = L_1 + L_2 + L_3 \ \ldots \ \text{etc.}$$

(2) Inductors in parallel:
$$L_{TOTAL} = \frac{1}{\dfrac{1}{L_1} + \dfrac{1}{L_2} + \dfrac{1}{L_3} \ \ldots \ \text{etc.}}$$

(3) Two inductors in parallel:

$$L_{TOTAL} = \frac{L_1 L_2}{L_1 + L_2}$$

(4) Coupled inductances in series with fields aiding:

$$L_{TOTAL} = L_1 + L_2 + 2M$$

(5) Coupled inductances in series with fields opposing:

$$L_{TOTAL} = L_1 + L_2 - 2M$$

(6) Coupled inductances in parallel with fields aiding:

$$L_{TOTAL} = \frac{1}{\dfrac{1}{L_1 + M} + \dfrac{1}{L_2 + M}}$$

(7) Coupled inductances in parallel with fields opposing:

$$L_{TOTAL} = \frac{1}{\dfrac{1}{L_1 - M} + \dfrac{1}{L_2 - M}}$$

(8) Mutual induction of two rf coils with fields interacting:

$$M = \frac{L_1 - L_2}{4}$$

Where

L_1 is the total inductance of both coils with fields aiding
L_2 is the total inductance of both coils with fields opposing

(9) Coupling coefficient of two rf coils inductively coupled so as to give transformer action:

$$K = \frac{M}{\sqrt{L_1 L_2}}$$

METER FORMULAS

(1) Ohms/volt $= \dfrac{1}{I}$

Where

I = Full scale current in amperes

(2) Meter resistance:

$$R_{METER} = \frac{E_{FULL\,SCALE}}{I_{FULL\,SCALE}}$$

(3) Current shunt:

$$R_{SHUNT} = \frac{R_{METER}}{N - 1}$$

Where
N is the new full-scale reading divided by the original full-scale reading (both in same units)

OHM'S LAW FOR DC CIRCUITS

(1) $I = \dfrac{E}{R}$

(2) $I = \sqrt{\dfrac{P}{R}}$

(3) $I = \dfrac{P}{E}$

(4) $R = \dfrac{E}{I}$

(5) $R = \dfrac{P}{I^2}$

(6) $R = \dfrac{E^2}{P}$

(7) $E = IR$

(8) $E = \dfrac{P}{I}$

(9) $E = \sqrt{PR}$

(10) $P = I^2R$

(11) $P = EI$

(12) $P = \dfrac{E^2}{R}$

OHM'S LAW FOR AC CIRCUITS

(1) $I = \dfrac{E}{Z}$

(2) $I = \sqrt{\dfrac{P}{Z \cos \theta}}$

(3) $I = \dfrac{P}{E \cos \theta}$

(4) $Z = \dfrac{E}{I}$

(5) $Z = \dfrac{P}{I^2 \cos \theta}$

(6) $Z = \dfrac{E^2 \cos \theta}{P}$

(7) $E = IZ$

(8) $E = \dfrac{P}{I \cos \theta}$

(9) $E = \sqrt{\dfrac{PZ}{\cos \theta}}$

(10) $P = I^2 Z \cos \theta$

(11) $P = IE \cos \theta$

(12) $P = \dfrac{E^2 \cos \theta}{Z}$

PEAK VALUE
(1) $V_{PEAK} = 1.414 \text{ (rms value)}$
(2) $V_{PEAK} = 1.570 \text{ (average value)}$

PEAK TO PEAK VALUE
(1) $V_{P-P} = 2.828 \text{ (rms value)}$
(2) $V_{P-P} = 3.140 \text{ (average value)}$

PHASE ANGLE
$\theta = \text{arc tan} \dfrac{X}{R}$

POWER FACTOR
(1) $\text{p.f.} = \cos \theta$
(2) $D = \cot \theta$

REACTANCE
(1) $X_L = 2\pi f L$
(2) $X_C = \dfrac{1}{2\pi f C}$

RESISTANCE

(1) Resistors in series:

$$R_{TOTAL} = R_1 + R_2 + R_3 \ldots \text{ etc.}$$

(2) Resistors in parallel:

$$R_{TOTAL} = \cfrac{1}{\cfrac{1}{R_1} + \cfrac{1}{R_2} + \cfrac{1}{R_3} \ldots \text{ etc.}}$$

(3) Two resistors in parallel:

$$R_{TOTAL} = \frac{R_1 R_2}{R_1 + R_2}$$

RESONANCE

(1) $f_{RESONANCE} = \dfrac{1}{2\pi\sqrt{LC}}$

(2) $L = \dfrac{1}{4\pi^2 f^2 C}$

(3) $C = \dfrac{1}{4\pi^2 f^2 L}$

RIGHT TRIANGLE

(1) $\sin \theta = \dfrac{O}{H}$

(2) $\cos \theta = \dfrac{A}{H}$

(3) $\tan \theta = \dfrac{O}{A}$

(4) $\sec \theta = \dfrac{H}{A}$

(5) $\cot \theta = \dfrac{A}{O}$

(6) $\csc \theta = \dfrac{H}{O}$

ROOT MEAN SQUARE (SINE WAVE SHAPE ONLY)

(1) rms = 0.707 (peak value)

(2) rms = 1.111 (average value)

SECANT

(1) $\sec \theta = \dfrac{H}{A}$

(2) $\sec \theta = \text{cosecant} \ (90 - \theta)$

(3) $\sec \theta = \dfrac{1}{\cos \theta}$

SINE

(1) $\sin \theta = \dfrac{O}{H}$

(2) $\sin \theta = \cos \ (90 - \theta)$

(3) $\sin \theta = \dfrac{1}{\text{cosecant} \ \theta}$

SUSCEPTANCE

(1) $B_L = \dfrac{X_L}{R_L{}^2 + X_L{}^2}$

(2) $B_C = \dfrac{1}{X_C}$

(3) $B_{TOTAL} = B_1 + B_2 + B_3 \ldots$ etc.

TANGENT

(1) $\tan \theta = \dfrac{O}{A}$

(2) $\tan \theta = \cot \ (90 - \theta)$

(3) $\tan \theta = \dfrac{1}{\cot \theta}$

TEMPERATURE

(1) $C = 0.556 \, F - 17.8$

(2) $F = 1.8 \, C + 32$

(3) $K = C + 273$

TRANSISTORS, BIPOLAR

(1) $I_c = I_b \, \beta$

(2) $I_e \cong I_c$

(3) $E_e = E_b - 0.7$ (silicon transistors)

(4) $E_e = E_b - 0.3$ (germanium transistors)

(5) $I_e = \dfrac{E_e}{R_e}$

(6) $Z_b = R_e \beta$

(7) $A_P = \beta$

Where:

A_P is the power gain of a common collector configuration

TRANSISTORS, FIELD EFFECT

$$G_{fs} = \frac{\Delta I_D}{\Delta V_{GS}}$$

Where:

G_{fs} is the transconductance value
ΔV_{GS} is a change in gate to source voltage
ΔI_D is a subsequent change in drain current

TRANSFORMER RATIO

$$\frac{N_p}{N_s} = \frac{E_p}{E_s} = \frac{I_s}{I_p} = \sqrt{\frac{Z_p}{Z_s}}$$

WAVELENGTH

$$\lambda = \frac{3 \times 10^8}{f}$$

Index